JERUSALEM
IN THE TIME OF
NEHEMIAH

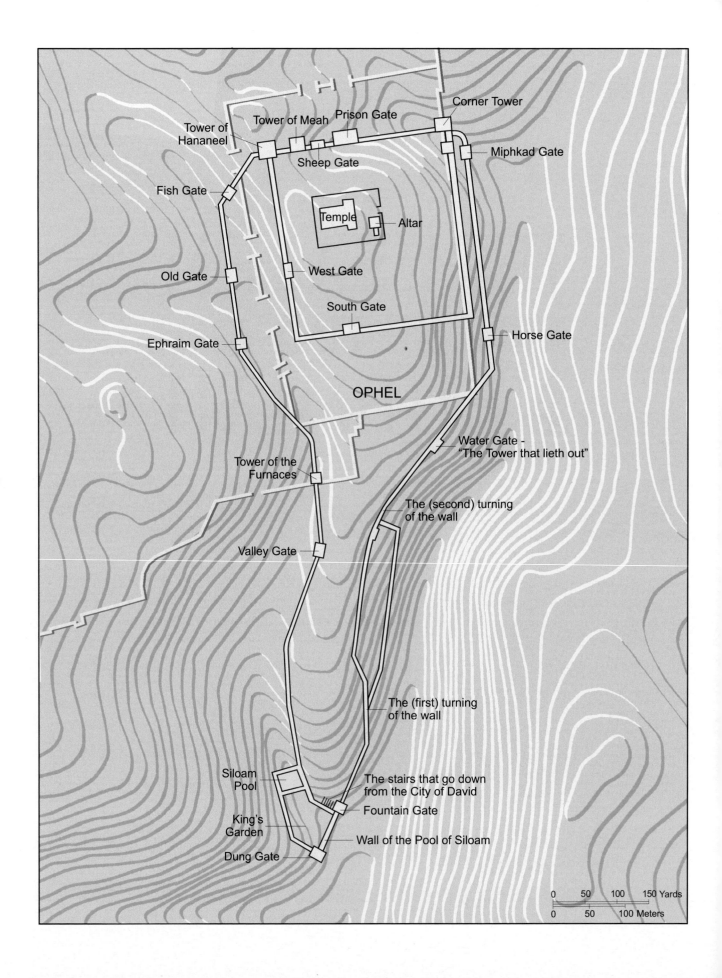

Leen & Kathleen Ritmeyer

JERUSALEM IN THE TIME OF NEHEMIAH

Carta, Jerusalem

Model of Nehemiah's Jerusalem designed and photographed by
Leen Ritmeyer
and constructed in 2003 by the Year 10 students of
Heritage College, Adelaide, Australia

Other illustrations courtesy of Leen Ritmeyer on
pp. 8–9, 12 (below), 27–28, 34, 36, 39–40, 42, 44–45, 46 (top), 51, 56–60, 64–67
Photographs of the model on pp. 64 and 66 by Philip Evans
p. 47 (bottom) courtesy of The Institute of Archaeology, Hebrew University of Jerusalem
All others from the archives of Carta, Jerusalem

First edition 2005
Copyright © 2005 by Carta, Jerusalem
18 Ha'uman Street, POB 2500, Jerusalem 91024, Israel
www.holyland-jerusalem.com
E-mail: carta@carta.co.il

Designed and produced by Carta, Jerusalem
Editor: Barbara Ball
Artwork: Leen Ritmeyer
Additional artwork: Evgeny Vasenin
Cartography: Carta, Jerusalem
Amnon Shmaya, Vladimir Shestakovsky
Cover: Irena Shnitman

Frontispiece: Map of Jerusalem in the Time of Nehemiah
(this and map on p. 26 based on research by Leen Ritmeyer)

ISBN: 965-220-556-7

Printed in Israel

CONTENTS

WRITTEN SOURCES FOR THE TIME OF NEHEMIAH

ANCIENT SOURCES

The Hebrew Scriptures   The books of Ezra, Nehemiah and Esther
                              The prophetical books of Haggai, Zechariah and Malachi

The stone inscriptions of Darius at Behistun, Iran (6th century B.C.)
Here on the ancient road connecting Babylon to Ecbatana, Darius the Great had a bas-relief carved on a rock face to commemorate his victory over the pseudo-Smerdis who wished to seize the Persian throne. Information about the division of the Empire into satrapies is also included in the long text of inscriptions, which are written in three languages: Akkadian, Old Persian and Elamite. In the early nineteenth century, the labours of the British Sir Henry Rawlinson resulted in the decipherment of the text, making it possible to read the numerous inscribed clay tablets that were later discovered in Nineveh.

Scylax of Caryanda (6th century B.C.)
Scylax was a sailor in the Persian service, who was commissioned by Darius the Great to explore the course of the Indus Valley. References in the works of other ancient writers such as Aristotle and Herodotus would indicate that he left a written record of his voyages. With the information he brought back, Darius was able to conquer the Indus Valley and expand his empire.

Herodotus of Halicarnassus (c. 484–420 B.C.)
Called by Cicero the "father of history," Herodotus was the first European (a Greek) to write a prose history of the ancient world. His account of the Greco-Persian wars in *The Histories* is the result of reference to other works, particularly the writings of Hecataeus, the geographer of Asia Minor, an especially enquiring mind which recorded oral traditions and wide travel throughout the Persian empire and beyond. As would be expected, his writings have a definite bias and are sometimes prone to exaggeration, but their easy style make them a pleasure to read and they are the leading primary source for this period.

Herodotus

Xenophon of Athens (c. 431–350 B.C.)
Exiled from his native city, Xenophon served on the expedition of Cyrus as a Greek mercenary. After the death of Cyrus, he became a commander of the Greek force, the "Ten Thousand", who fought for the Persians. The account of his exploits is contained in his *Anabasis*. His other writings include *Hellenica*, a history of Greece, of which the first two books are a continuation of the work of Thucydides, who wrote *The Peloponnesian War*.

Diodorus Siculus (1st century B.C.)
Diodorus was a Greek historian from Agyrium in Sicily. His *Biblioteca Historia* was written in 40 books, only some of which have survived intact. It is especially useful as a source for the lost works of earlier writers.

Xenophon

MODERN WRITINGS

Charles Rollin, *The Ancient History of Egyptians, Carthaginians, Assyrians, Babylonians, Medes and Persians, Grecians and Macedonians* (first published in French, 12 vols, Paris, 1730–1738, numerous English editions. We used the 6-volume edition printed in London in 1850 for Longman).

Benjamin Mazar, *The Mountain of the Lord* (New York, Doubleday and Co., 1975).

Yohanan Aharoni, *The Land of the Bible: A Historical Geography* (Philadelphia, Westminister Press, 1979).

Nahman Avigad, *Discovering Jerusalem* (Nashville, Thomas Nelson, 1983).

James Purvis, revised by Eric Meyers, in Hershel Shanks (ed.), *Ancient Israel*, revised and expanded edition, "Exile and Return: From the Babylonian Destruction to the Reconstruction of the Jewish State" (Washington, Biblical Archaeology Society, 1999).

Ephraim Stern, *Archaeology of the Land of the Bible: The Assyrian, Babylonian, and Persian Periods (732–332 B.C.E.)*, Vol. 2 (Anchor Bible, 2001).

Jerusalem had been forsaken under the cruelty of the Babylonians. Its exiles returned under the beneficence of the Persians. What had changed? Everything had changed for Jerusalem. The Lamentations of Jeremiah describes it thus:

The LORD hath purposed to destroy the wall of the daughter of Zion: he hath stretched out a line, he hath not withdrawn his hand from destroying: therefore he made the rampart and the wall to lament; they languished together.

Her gates are sunk into the ground; he hath destroyed and broken her bars.

(Lam. 2:8–9)

The city was a reproach to her people. It had reached its greatest extent under the Judean kings, just over a century

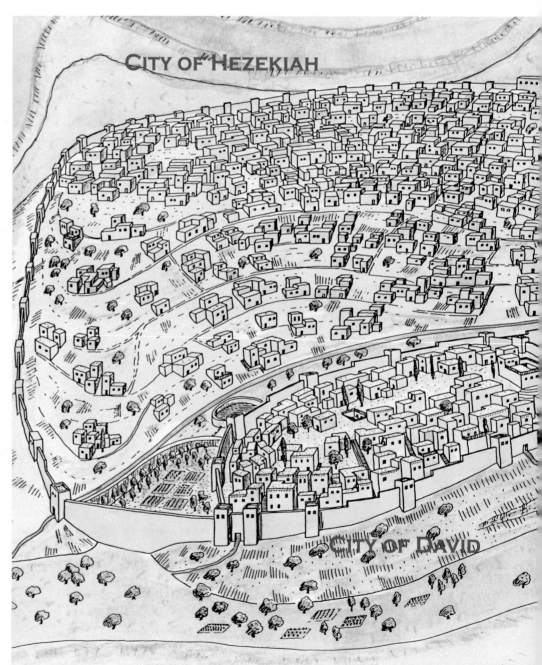

"Jerusalem is builded as a city that is compact (joined) together."

(Psalm 122:3)

earlier. Now, the whole city with its great Broad Wall built by King Hezekiah lay in ruins. Piles of soot and ash mixed with the rubble of the walls and here and there arrowheads of both the conquering Babylonian army and the Israelite defenders bore witness to the violent destruction of the city in 586 B.C.

Such was the picture of Jerusalem as described to Nehemiah in the palace of Shushan by another Israelite:

And they said unto me, The remnant that are left of the captivity there in the province are in great affliction and reproach: the wall of Jerusalem also is broken down, and the gates thereof are burned with fire. (Neh. 1:3)

But who was Nehemiah and what was he doing in the Persian palace? Charles Rollin (London, 1850) writes of him:

Nehemiah was also a Jew, of distinguished merit and piety, and one of the cup-bearers to King Artaxerxes. This was a very considerable employment in

A group of arrowheads from the time of the Babylonian destruction of Jerusalem, found at the foot of an Israelite tower in the Jewish Quarter excavations. The three leaf-shaped iron arrowheads would have been used by the Israelites, while the triple-bladed socketed bronze arrowhead is of the type used by foreign mercenaries fighting for the Babylonian army.

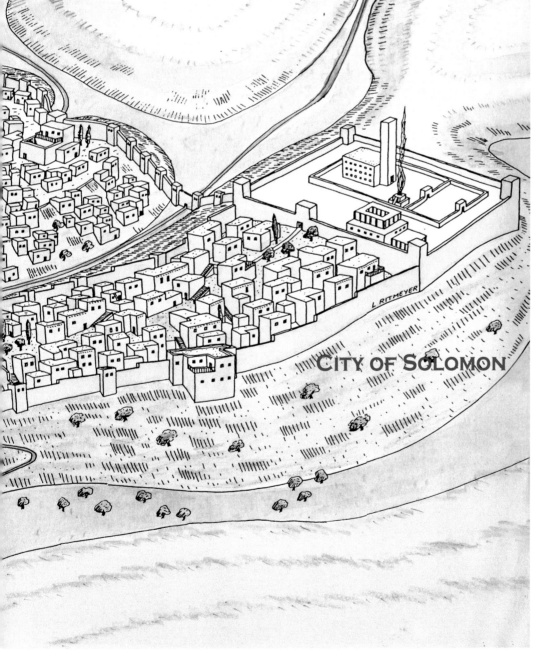

CITY OF SOLOMON

L. RITMEYER

the Persian court, because of the privilege annexed to it, of being often near the king's person and of being allowed to speak to him in the most favourable moments. (Vol II, Book VII, p.447)

Herodotus called the position of cup-bearer, one "of no trifling honour" (*Histories* III.34).

We were now in the second historical succession of empires as depicted in Nebuchadnezzar's Dream. Here, the Medo-Persian Empire is portrayed as the breast and arms of silver, in contrast to the head of gold (representing the Babylonian Empire under Nebuchadnezzar).

The realm was divided into large provinces or satrapies, each governed by a satrap appointed by the Persian king. As part of their benevolent policy, however, the Persians, wherever they could, ruled through the administrative apparatus put in place during the time of the Assyrian

and Babylonian empires. As Yohanan Aharoni wrote:

Within the Persian governmental framework considerable autonomy was allowed to the various provinces, and many of the governors were descendants of the local nobility.
(Philadelphia 1979, p.357)

Thus Nehemiah, with his heart still in Zion, was a natural choice for governor of the province of Judah or Yehud, part of the fifth satrapy of Abar Nahara or Beyond the River.

But let us journey back through the main events that brought us to this day. The Book of Nehemiah was only one of a series of books about this period that made it into the Jewish canon of Scriptures. The books of Ezra, which was originally paired with Nehemiah in the same book, Esther and the prophets Haggai and Zechariah, all concern themselves with the great time of Jewish

The elders and the virgins of Jerusalem lament the desolation of the city, as it is written: "The elders of the daughter of Zion sit upon the ground, and keep silence: they have cast up dust upon their heads; they have girded themselves with sackcloth: the virgins of Jerusalem hang down their heads to the ground." (Lam. 2:10)

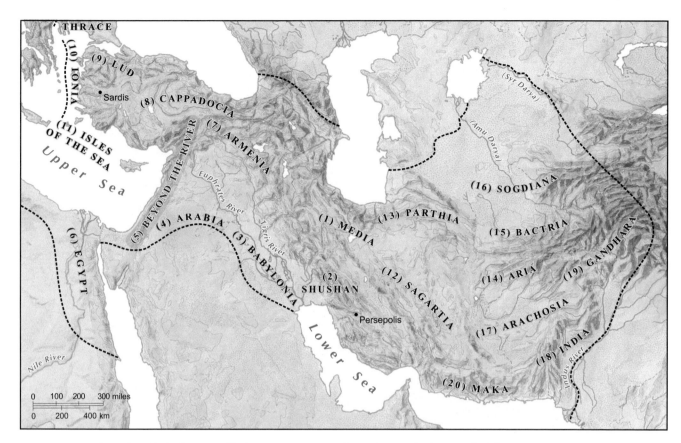

The map shows the satrapies of the Persian Empire with the following labeled regions:

THRACE
(10) IONIA
(9) LUD
Sardis
(8) CAPPADOCIA
(11) ISLES OF THE SEA
Upper Sea
(7) ARMENIA
(5) BEYOND THE RIVER
Euphrates River
Tigris River
(4) ARABIA
(3) BABYLONIA
(6) EGYPT
Nile River
(1) MEDIA
(2) SHUSHAN
Persepolis
(13) PARTHIA
(12) SAGARTIA
Lower Sea
(16) SOGDIANA
(Syr Darya)
(Amu Darya)
(15) BACTRIA
(14) ARIA
(19) GANDHARA
(17) ARACHOSIA
(18) INDIA
Indus River
(20) MAKA

0 100 200 300 miles
0 200 400 km

restoration after the Babylonian Exile. In the past, Bible critics have challenged the order of events in the books of Ezra and Nehemiah. Recently, however, the traditional sequence as presented in the books has regained acceptance.

538 B.C. Edict of Cyrus. King Cyrus II the Great (539–530 B.C.) permits the return to Jerusalem of the Jewish exiles in Babylon, thus defining the status of Judah as a province:

> Now in the first year of Cyrus king of Persia, that the word of the LORD by the mouth of Jeremiah might be fulfilled, the LORD stirred up the spirit of Cyrus king of Persia, that he made a proclamation throughout all his kingdom, and put it also in writing, saying,
>
> Thus saith Cyrus king of Persia, The LORD God of heaven hath given me all the kingdoms of the earth; and he hath charged me to build him an house at Jerusalem, which is in Judah.
>
> Who is there among you of all his people? His God be with him, and let him go up to Jerusalem, which is in Judah, and build the house of the LORD God of Israel, (he is the God,) which is in Jerusalem. (Ezra 1:1–3)

This was a manifestation of the policy Cyrus adopted throughout the empire he had conquered: to restore temples and to return to their homelands the various peoples who had been exiled to Babylon by earlier kings. King Cyrus himself came from the Achaemenid Dynasty which had ruled the small kingdom of Anshan, in what is now southwestern Iran.

The first group of exiles returned to Jerusalem under Zerubbabel (a descendant of Jehoiachin, the last king of Judah) and Jeshua the priest. They managed to set up the altar and lay the foundation of the temple (Ezra 3:2,10).

529 B.C. A letter is sent to the Persian king by the Samaritans opposing the restoration of Jerusalem and its temple (Ezra 4:1,6–7).

The satrapies of the Persian Empire under Darius I (biblical Ahasuerus), who "reigned from India even unto Ethiopia, over an hundred and seven and twenty provinces" (Esther 1:1).

King Cyrus the Great.

11

(right) This clay cylinder, inscribed in Babylonian cuneiform, gives an account of how Cyrus, King of Persia (549–530 B.C.), took Babylon in a bloodless victory. This had been prophesied 164 years earlier by the prophet Isaiah (45:1–5): "Thus saith the LORD to his anointed, to Cyrus, whose right hand I have holden, to subdue nations before him; and I will loose the loins of kings, to open before him the two leaved gates; and the gates shall not be shut;

"I will go before thee, and make the crooked places straight: I will break in pieces the gates of brass, and cut in sunder the bars of iron:

"And I will give thee the treasures of darkness, and hidden riches of secret places, that thou mayest know that I, the LORD, which call thee by thy name, am the God of Israel.

"For Jacob my servant's sake, and Israel mine elect, I have even called thee by thy name: I have surnamed thee, though thou hast not known me."

The cylinder also records his humane policy of returning to their lands the peoples deported by the Babylonians and aiding them in the restoration of the worship of their gods. It has sometimes been described as "the first charter of human rights."

(below) This tomb at Pasargadae in southern Iran, is thought to be that of Cyrus the Great. Pasargadae ("camp of the Persians") was the capital of Persia, until Darius built a new capital at Persepolis.

522 B.C. The building of the Temple ceased by order of King Cambyses (529–522 B.C.; Ezra 4:23–24). The son of Cyrus the Great, he had disposed of his brother Smerdis in order to gain unchallenged rule.

521 B.C. While Cambyses is in Egypt, a Median impostor, Gaumata, claims to be the true Smerdis, raises a revolt, and rules for seven months. Darius, the son of Hystaspes, the satrap of Parthia and of a collateral branch of the royal family, kills Gaumata and assumes the throne.

520 B.C. The original Edict of Cyrus, permitting the rebuilding of the Temple, is discovered in Ecbatana by King Darius (522–486) and reaffirmed by him in the second year of his reign (Ezra 6). Darius (and later his son Xerxes) builds a new ceremonial capital in Persepolis, but Susa (Shushan the palace) remains the political capital. The name Susa is thought to be derived from the Persian for water lilies, said to have grown in lakes and swamps outside the city. The government would move to mountainous Ecbatana in summer.

In the same year the prophets Haggai and Zechariah begin to prophesy to the Israelites, who had lost heart in the face of the opposition. They speak of a glorious future for Jerusalem, promising that the temple would be completed, even though, in comparison to the Temple of Solomon, it would be a "day of small things" (Zech. 4:10).

The message of Haggai to Zerubbabel and Joshua was heard: "Who is left among you that saw this house in her first glory? and how do ye see it now? is it not in your eyes in comparison of it as nothing?" (Haggai 2:3)

519 B.C. The Feast of Ahasuerus (Esther 1:3).

Now it came to pass in the days of Ahasuerus (this is Ahasuerus which reigned, from India even unto Ethiopia, over an hundred and seven and twenty provinces). (Esther 1:1)

Ahasuerus can be identified with Darius Hystaspes, as he was the only Persian king who ruled over a territory which extended from India to Ethiopia. The name Ahasuerus must be regarded more as a title than a name, as it signifies "possessor" (*ahaz*) and (*ve*) "head" (*rosh*).

Using Plutarch and Pliny as his sources, Charles Rollin makes a most enlightening observation on the Persian monarchical government:

Those people paid extraordinary honours to the prince on the throne. because in his person they respected the character of the Deity, whose image and viceregent he was with regards to

This now headless statue of Darius the Great was carved in Egypt but later brought to the great palace in Susa, where it was discovered in 1972. It is the only freestanding sculpture from ancient Persia, most of the other representations being made on relief carvings. Among other inscriptions made on this statue is that inscribed in hieroglyphics on the belt which reads: "I am Darius, the great king, king of kings, king of all people, king in this great earth far and wide, the son of Hystaspes, an Achaemenid."

them, being placed on the throne by the hands of the supreme governor of the world, and invested with his authority and power, in order to be the minister of his providence, and the dispenser of his goodness towards the people.

(Vol II, Book IV, p.115)

This makes Vashti's decision to disobey her husband all the more astounding (Esther 1:12).

The story of Esther also illustrates one of the most notable achievements of the Persians under Darius—their postal system. Darius is recorded in Esther 1:22 as sending letters to all the king's provinces in a bid to prevent the negative example of his wife's disobedience from spreading. Herodotus, impressed by this efficient system, described it in glowing terms:

There is nothing mortal which accomplishes a journey with more speed than these messengers, so skillfully has this been invented by the Persians. For they say that according to the number of days of which the entire journey consists, so many horses and men are set at intervals, each man and horse appointed for a day's journey. Neither snow nor rain nor heat nor darkness of night prevents them from accomplishing the task proposed to them with the very utmost speed. The first one rides and delivers the message with which he is charged to the second, and the second to the third; and after that it goes through them handed from one to the other, as in the torch race among the Greeks, which they perform for Hephaestus. This kind of running of their horses the Persians call angareion. (Histories 8.98)

515 B.C. The dedication of the Jerusalem Temple in the sixth year of Darius's reign, seventy years after the destruction of Jerusalem and the Temple in 586 B.C. The Chronicler, thought to be Ezra, wrote that this was allowed to happen in order:

To fulfil the word of the LORD by the mouth of Jeremiah, until the land had enjoyed her sabbaths: for as long as she lay desolate she kept sabbath, to fulfil threescore and ten years. (2 Chr 36:21)

Ben Sira extolled those responsible for its construction in the Apocryphal book of Ecclesiasticus in the famous passage, "Let us praise illustrious men" (Ecclesiasticus 44:1):

How shall we extol Zerubbabel?
He was like as a signet ring on the right hand, so too was Jeshua son of Jozadak;
they who in their days built the temple, and raised to the Lord a holy people, destined to everlasting glory.

(Ecclesiasticus 49:11–12)

However, to those who had seen the temple that had been destroyed by the Babylonians, it was a disappointment.

514 B.C. The marriage of Esther to King Darius in the seventh year of his reign (Esther 2:16). Esther was the young cousin of the Jew Mordecai, who had been carried away captive from Jerusalem in 596 B.C. during the reign of Jehoiachin. Chosen for her special qualities from a large number of young virgins when Vashti refused to show her beauty, her marriage to the king had been delayed, presumably because of his occupation with military matters.

509 B.C. The powerful Haman the Agagite plots to kill all Jews throughout the Persian Empire. They are dramatically saved by Esther, who has become queen and who follows the advice of Mordecai. In a reversal of plot, Haman and his sons are hanged and Mordecai is exalted. The Feast of Purim (Lots) is instituted to commemorate the deliverance of the Jews and they are instructed to keep it year by year. A New Testament reference to the feast is found in John 5:1.

485–465 B.C. Reign of Xerxes I, the son of Darius the Great and Atossa, daughter of Cyrus the Great. Egypt rebels against their Persian masters with the death of Darius and this would

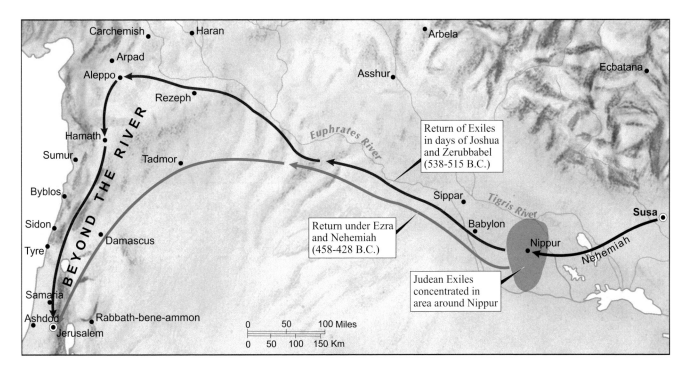

Return of Exiles
in days of Joshua
and Zerubbabel
(538-515 B.C.)

Return under Ezra
and Nehemiah
(458-428 B.C.)

Judean Exiles
concentrated in
area around Nippur

BEYOND THE RIVER

Euphrates River

Tigris River

Nehemiah

Carchemish •Haran •Arbela Ecbatana.
•Arpad
Aleppo •
Rezeph•
Hamath • Asshur.
Sumur• Tadmor•
Byblos• Sippar•
Sidon• Babylon• Susa ⊙
Tyre• Damascus Nippur•
Samaria•
Ashdod• •Rabbath-bene-ammon
⊙Jerusalem

0   50   100 Miles
0   50   100   150 Km

have been the background to the new allegations made against the Jews who were building in Jerusalem. Xerxes swiftly subjugates the country, removing to Susa the statue of Darius (see illustration) that had been erected in Heliopolis. For the next forty years, the southern border of the Persian Empire in Egypt is protected by Jewish soldiers at Elephantine (Yeb), located near Aswan. Their settlement there dated from before the days of King Cambyses.

The Persian War against the Greeks continues under the reign of Xerxes. Darius lost the Battle of Marathon (490 B.C.) and Xerxes was defeated by the Greeks at Salamis (480 B.C.). He is slain by the captain of his bodyguard and succeeded by his son, Artaxerxes Longimanus.

465–425 B.C. Reign of Artaxerxes I (nicknamed Longimanus, meaning "Long-handed").

458 B.C. Artaxerxes commissions Ezra the scribe to go on a mission of inquiry in his seventh year and to beautify the Temple at Jerusalem (Ezra 7). Ezra leads the group of exiles from Babylon, sets the affairs of the Jews in order through a series of reforms and re-establishes the priesthood in Jerusalem.

444 B.C. Nehemiah obtains the permission of King Artaxerxes (in the twentieth year of his reign) to return to Jerusalem and to rebuild its walls. The reference to "the queen also sitting by him (the king)" (Neh 2:6), may refer to Esther as queen mother sitting by her grandson, as the king's harem would also accommodate the revered, older widowed women as well as the wives and concubines of the reigning king.

Nehemiah rebuilds the walls and gates of Jerusalem (in 52 days), overcoming the opposition of Sanballat of Samaria, Tobiah the Ammonite and Geshem the Arabian (Neh. 1–7).

Nehemiah calls an assembly to prevent the exploitation of the Jewish poor by some of the Jewish nobles who were charging exorbitant rates of interest and seizing their land (Neh. 5).

Nehemiah refuses to accept the generous food allowance granted to him as governor, unlike his predecessors. Of his own resources, he provides meals daily for 150 Jews, apart from those from surrounding nations (Neh. 5).

The return of the Jews from exile:

538 B.C. (Ezra 1–6)— Return under Joshua and Zerubbabel; the first group of returnees rebuild the temple.

458 B.C. (Ezra 7–10)— Return under Ezra; the second group restore the Mosaic Law.

444 B.C. (Neh. 1–12)— Return under Nehemiah; the third group rebuild the walls of Jerusalem.

Nehemiah appoints gatekeepers, singers, and Levites to protect the city (Neh. 7). Ezra (in the presence of Nehemiah) reads the law to the assembled Israelites at the Water Gate in Jerusalem. The Feast of Tabernacles is kept and the covenant renewed (Neh. 8–10). Lots are cast to bring one in ten Israelites to live in Jerusalem to strengthen the city (Neh. 11).

Nehemiah leads a ceremony to dedicate the new wall. Two companies of singers and instrumentalists walk in opposite directions, beginning and ending at the Prison Gate on the north side of the city (Neh. 12).

432 B.C. Nehemiah leaves Jerusalem after a twelve-year stay and returns to Persia (Neh. 5:14, 13:6). Nehemiah then returns to Jerusalem and introduces reforms concerning intermarriage sometime before the end of the reign of Artaxerxes Longimanus.

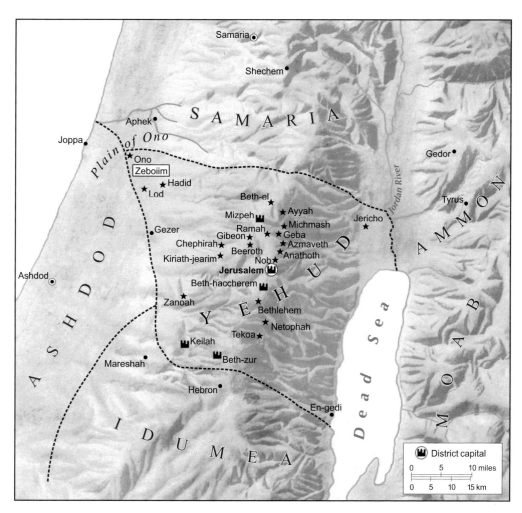

Map of the land of Judah (Yehud) in the time of the Return to Zion.

The list of Judah's adversaries in the Book of Nehemiah (2:19, 4:7) informs us about its neighboring provinces. Sanballat was governor of the province of Samaria to the north and feared the diminishing of his power if Jerusalem was rebuilt. Mount Gerizim would also have been in competition with Jerusalem as a center of worship. Sanballat's name and that of two of his descendants are mentioned in papyri written in Aramaic and found in Elephantine (Cowley #30).

The name of Tobiah the Ammonite is mentioned in two hall inscriptions found in caves eleven miles west of Amman. That of Geshem the Arabian has been identified in a Lihyanhite Arabic inscription from Dedan in northwestern Arabia dated to the fifth century B.C. Unnamed Ashdodites were also mentioned among those that tried to demoralize Nehemiah.

Both Ezra (2:1–34) and Nehemiah (7:6–38) list the names of the exiles who returned to Judah and the towns from which they came. The list of the builders in Nehemiah 3 also indicates those towns that were administrative centers.

> Great too is the memory of Nehemiah, who rebuilt our walls which lay in ruins, erected the gates and bars and rebuilt our houses.
>
> (Ecclesiasticus 49:13)

Ben-Sira's commendation of Nehemiah in his "Let us praise illustrious men" passage which begins in Ecclesiasticus 44:1.

The distribution of Yehud coins (top) and stamps (above) accords with the map of settlements of Jewish returnees to Judah. The Jews were granted permission to make their own coinage and copied the Attic coin with its owl symbol, adding the letters Yehud to distinguish them from the coins of other provinces.

These letters were also stamped onto jar-handles, such as those of wine-jars and these are the most common finds from the Persian Period in Israel. A plethora of them were found in stratum 9 (the Persian period) of the City of David excavations in Jerusalem. The seals are often marked with the symbol or name of a district governor.

The Story of Ashur—An Imaginative Reconstruction

There it was, our village of Tekoa, looming like a fortress in the midst of the desert landscape. It was still morning, as we had left Jerusalem after only a few hours' sleep, to do this thing we both dreaded. My companion was Ethnan, another of the men of Tekoa and the road we had to take was a good one, as it was an important route along the watershed of the Judean hills. Being the month of Elul, as it was, the sky was a deep calm blue, with each feature standing out against its background as if carved with a knife. The fields we passed should have been full to harvest, but the fruit we saw had not reached full size because of the terrible drought. Only the figs were full and luscious as they can tolerate complete dryness. Even the pomegranates, which usually bejewel the entire countryside, were small and mean as though holding back on their rosy loveliness.

Tekoa was a true outpost toward the desert, situated on a high ridge surrounded on three sides by a deep canyon. Through this canyon ran the brook Tekoa which led east to the Dead Sea. Down in these valleys were caves so ancient that nobody knew who was the first person to live in them.

High above this awesome deep, on the slopes which descended from the cluster of houses that made up our village, lay our vineyards. Defying the desert, they covered the slanting hills for a long distance on all sides of the ridge. As our mules carried us nearer to Tekoa, our own vineyard came plainly into view. There was its watchtower: there the walls I had so painstakingly constructed from stones cleared out of the field. And there were the vines with the grapes almost ready to be harvested. It looked like a good crop this year, despite the drought. We had brought water from our cistern to water the base of the vines earlier in the season because of the lack of rain. But this year, someone else's family would eat the fruit, tread the grapes, ferment the wine and reap the profit. We had come to mortgage our vineyard — unthinkable, but there appeared to be no way out!

Coming towards us now was one of the nobles of our village who did not respond to Nehemiah's call: "Come and let us build up the wall of Jerusalem, that we be no more a reproach." Their sort did not seem to be sorry that the walls of the city lay in ruins around a temple that had taken so long to build. Their sole aim was to profit from the crisis conditions and to buy up land as cheaply as possible. This was what Beriah planned to do with me. He knew that I had no choice but to sell him my vineyard. My family back in Jerusalem needed food and because I was busy with the rest of the Tekoites building the wall, I could not tend to my vineyard and earn what was coming to me from a year's work. The labour of the different seasons came flooding into my mind: how we had cut back the vine branches after last year's vintage, how we had collected dung to fertilize it, how we had mended any breaches in the walls (just like we were doing now in Jerusalem), how we had repaired the watchtower and, hardest of all, how we had pruned every branch until our wrists ached. But what did this noble care? He would soon own half the village. Other wretched souls would come on a similar mission after my short time away from building the walls of Jerusalem.

We talk money. I didn't expect much because of the hard times, but such a mean sum? And I can't even hope for the vineyard to be returned to me in the Jubilee Year. This wonderful law which stipulates that property be returned in the fiftieth year to its original owner, who was forced by poverty to sell it, has hardly ever been observed. What is there for all my labour? But, I will be able to buy some corn for my family, so that we may have some bread to eat. If I can just get some of our oil from the house, we will be alright.

A quick visit to our little home to take a flagon of oil from the large stone jar in our kitchen and some things the children have asked for and we are on our way again. I cannot bear to turn back and look at the vineyard that is

now lost to me. We had returned from Babylon with Ezra just fourteen years before, full of hope that the Judean land of plenty described by my father's father could once again be restored. For me, who had been born in that strange land and whose father had vineyards on land he leased from the Babylonians in Nippur, to grow my own grapes on land that was my own was a wonderful thing. My father had called me Ashur, after our first ancestor in Tekoa and prayed that his son might one day return to claim what was rightfully his. And to think that it was our brethren, also men of Tekoa, who were taking it from us. My heart was hardened towards them like a stone.

But the good hand of our God was upon us also on our return journey. We could easily have been ambushed by raiders from some of the hostile provinces that now surrounded Judea, particularly the Idumeans who had seized the area of the Judean hills south of Beth-zur, our district capital, during the captivity.

And then the form of Jerusalem loomed into view. What a sight! How my heart thrilled to it! All around, the ruined walls were being built up so that now the complete outline of the city could be seen. Each section was being built by a different group. Riding up the Bethlehem road into the city, I passed by a group from Tekoa that was busy repairing the wall between

Tekoa as viewed from the east, with the fields of Tekoa in the foreground. The ancient settlement is located on the hilltop. A nineteenth-century illustration.

the Fish Gate and the Old Gate. I had to tell them the price I received for my vineyard. You could see from their pained looks what they thought of this! I stopped inside the gate to buy the prized corn from merchants who were also doing well from the situation. Crossing the city to my own family group, I passed by the temple built by Joshua and Zerubbabel. I had never seen the great Temple, destroyed by Nebuchadnezzar, but the older people said that the new one paled in comparison. But for me, who had promised in Babylon: "If I forget thee, O Jerusalem, let my right hand forget her cunning. If I do not remember thee, let my tongue cleave to the roof of my mouth; if I prefer not Jerusalem above my chief joy," to see the temple rebuilt, even if it lacked the magnificence of that of Solomon, was the crown of all my rejoicing. Even now, with all this frantic building activity, the

(center) Rebuilding the walls of Jerusalem.

ritual of the sanctuary went on continually. The smoke ascending from the altar was a constant background to our construction work.

As I rode, I kept a close eye out for our enemies (for the city concealed many) who could be following us. My group were building from the great tower that lay out as far as the Horse Gate. Since Nehemiah charged us to stay within the city walls, we all slept beside the section of the wall that we were building. My family was living in one of the houses that were still standing after the Babylonian destruction. You could hardly call it a house — it had been derelict for over one hundred years. Soot from the Babylonian conflagration still clung to its walls and the frames of its doors and windows

hung wildly on their hinges until we could fix them. Others of us slept behind the city wall, with one of the group on guard day and night.

My wife was overjoyed to see me, as was the wife of Ethnan. And our five children were delighted with the things I had brought from Tekoa, some little thing for each one of them. Naarah immediately wanted the corn put in

her makeshift kitchen and started to measure it out, knead the dough and prepare some unleavened bread. We had no patience to wait for the dough to rise. The aroma of bread baking on the hotplate over the fire (of course, we had no proper oven) filled the house and was reward enough for our journey. "But the vineyard," Naarah said, "why must we lose our vineyard?" I comforted her with the words, "Our God is able to do all things — nothing is impossible for him." When we gave thanks for the food she put on the table, we felt that we had never understood the import of the words

A view from the Cave of Chariton of the canyon through which the brook Tekoa runs down to the Dead Sea. A nineteenth-century illustration.

before. Over the meal, the family spoke of others who were running out of money for food and also to pay the king's tribute. Nehemiah's relief of those that would otherwise have gone hungry was mentioned many times. Imagine—he fed 150 Jews at his table every day, apart from the people of the surrounding nations, who were also affected by the drought (they must have had a lot to think about—this Jewish governor caring about them!).

Then strengthened by our simple meal, it was back to the great work! Hepher was mighty relieved to see me arrive, as it meant that he could switch from building the wall to the job of standing guard. This was tense work, not knowing when the enemy could strike, but at least it gave you an opportunity to stand up straight for a while as you held the spear which was all that stood between us and those that wanted to stop us. I also kept my sword strapped on as I builded. It was cumbersome work but we became accustomed to it. We had already been laboring for many weeks in this manner. Supply of building stones was not a problem; there were piles of them left in the rubble from the walls that the Babylonians destroyed. And of course, we combined fieldstones with the dressed stones. We did not have the luxury of ordering dressed stones from the quarries and having them transported over a long distance. It seemed to us that

we had to work faster than any other wall-builders in history.

In some parts of our area, the wall was only breached and so it was just a matter of repairing the gaping holes that invited the enemy inside. Some parts were completely destroyed and we had to rebuild the wall to its full height. We used strings, one on either side of the wall and held between stones that were placed at intervals to mark the width of the wall. Once one course of stones and mortar was laid, the string was raised to the next layer of stones. This gave the wall a good straight line and the wall was kept precisely vertical by using a plumb-bob.

We had almost completed our assigned area and all around us, we could see that others also had almost finished their portion of the wall. Having done my required hours of building, I would normally have held the spear to protect the other Tekoites while they builded. But, I suddenly thought of Ephratah, my next-door neighbor in Tekoa. As I had passed the other Tekoite group when entering the city, I noticed him looking dejected and downcast. I knew that he had no land to sell and could sense his dejection that as a craftsman, he was not able to feed his family properly.

Recrossing the city, I heard a cry coming from a woman in one of the other building groups. It turned out that her family had been in such dire straits that they had actually sold one of their daughters into slavery in order to obtain some money. Now, they could hardly bring themselves to eat the food which they had bought with her price. Just before reaching the other Tekoite building group, more crying reached us. This time, it was a family lamenting the loss of their entire family estate that they had been forced to sell. But there was Ephratah with his wife, speaking to one of the nobles while resting his hands on the shoulders of his much-loved elder son, Caleb. I knew how much he loved his son, who had hands like him and could shape wood to his will. Coming closer, I saw the hated noble take some money out of his bag to give to Ephratah. Knowing that something awful was about to happen, I broke into a sprint and reaching Ephratah, told him: "Don't do it! Here, take what you need from this," opening my own bag with the money that was left in it. I managed to prevent this one terrible wrong, but the very thought of almost having done this caused the female members of the family to break into pitiful wailing. It seemed as though there was crying the entire length of the city walls.

Nobody could remain unmoved — how could we finish the work with such sadness in the city? But, of course, Nehemiah also could not fail to hear the cry. You could see his anger against the profiteers mounting. He moved between the different groups accompanied by the trumpeter whose job it was to sound the alarm. He listened to their stories. Once he understood the full extent of what was happening, he appeared to go deep within himself. We tried to guess what he would do. After a period of reflection, he called for a full assembly of the nobles and rulers. And then, by sheer force of a personality driven by the fear of God, he rebuked them with a voice that had to be obeyed. He reminded them that they were Jews, many of whom had been saved from Babylon. How could they treat their brethren as merchandise? How could they bring the reproach of the nations round about on God's people? He commanded them to restore all of the things that we had been forced to sell in our despair. We would get our lands, our vineyards, our houses, and most precious of all, our sons and our daughters back. And the family of Ashur would get their vineyard back as well. Our God, who had promised to fight for us, had kept his promise.

But now — back to that "great work," all of us feeling complete again. A few more hours' work and all the walls would be completed "with no breach left therein." And in fifty-two days, the wall was builded. So you see, I had to tell you my story, as I built with Nehemiah and who had ever heard of such a thing before?

THE BOOK OF NEHEMIAH — CHAPTER 3

1 Then Eliashib the high priest rose up with his brethren the priests, and they builded the sheep gate; they sanctified it, and set up the doors of it; even unto the tower of Meah they sanctified it, unto the tower of Hananeel.

2 And next unto him builded the men of Jericho. And next to them builded Zaccur the son of Imri.

3 But the fish gate did the sons of Hassenaah build, who also laid the beams thereof, and set up the doors thereof, the locks thereof, and the bars thereof.

4 And next unto them repaired Meremoth the son of Urijah, the son of Koz. And next unto them repaired Meshullam the son of Berechiah, the son of Meshezabeel. And next unto them repaired Zadok the son of Baana.

5 And next unto them the Tekoites repaired; but their nobles put not their necks to the work of their LORD.

6 Moreover the old gate repaired Jehoiada the son of Paseah, and Meshullam the son of Besodeiah; they laid the beams thereof, and set up the doors thereof, and the locks thereof, and the bars thereof.

7 And next unto them repaired Melatiah the Gibeonite, and Jadon the Meronothite, the men of Gibeon, and of Mizpah, unto the throne of the governor on this side the river.

8 Next unto him repaired Uzziel the son of Harhaiah, of the goldsmiths. Next unto him also repaired Hananiah the son of one of the apothecaries, and they fortified Jerusalem unto the broad wall.

9 And next unto them repaired Rephaiah the son of Hur, the ruler of the half part of Jerusalem.

10 And next unto them repaired Jedaiah the son of Harumaph, even over against his house.And next unto him repaired Hattush the son of Hashabniah.

11 Malchijah the son of Harim, and Hashub the son of Pahathmoab, repaired the other piece, and the tower of the furnaces.

12 And next unto him repaired Shallum the son of Halohesh, the ruler of the half part of Jerusalem, he and his daughters.

13 The valley gate repaired Hanun, and the inhabitants of Zanoah; they built it, and set up the doors thereof, the locks thereof, and the bars thereof, and a thousand cubits on the wall unto the dung gate.

14 But the dung gate repaired Malchiah the son of Rechab, the ruler of part of Bethhaccerem; he built it, and set up the doors thereof, the locks thereof, and the bars thereof.

15 But the gate of the fountain repaired Shallun the son of Colhozeh, the ruler of part of Mizpah; he built it, and covered it, and set up the doors thereof, the locks thereof, and the bars thereof, and the wall of the pool of Siloah by the king's garden, and unto the stairs that go down from the city of David.

16 After him repaired Nehemiah the son of Azbuk, the ruler of the half part of Bethzur, unto the place over against the sepulchres of David, and to the pool that was made, and unto the house of the mighty.

17 After him repaired the Levites, Rehum the son of Bani. Next unto him repaired Hashabiah, the ruler of the half part of Keilah, in his part.

18 After him repaired their brethren, Bavai the son of Henadad, the ruler of the half part of Keilah.

19 And next to him repaired Ezer the son of Jeshua, the ruler of Mizpah, another piece over against the going up to the armory at the turning of the wall.

20 After him Baruch the son of Zabbai earnestly repaired the other piece, from the turning of the wall unto the door of the house of Eliashib the high priest.

21 After him repaired Meremoth the son of Urijah the son of Koz another piece, from the door of the house of Eliashib even to the end of the house of Eliashib.

22 And after him repaired the priests, the men of the plain.

23 After him repaired Benjamin and Hashub over against their house. After him repaired Azariah the son of Maaseiah the son of Ananiah by his house.

24 After him repaired Binnui the son of Henadad another piece, from the house of Azariah unto the turning of the wall, even unto the corner.

25 Palal the son of Uzai, over against the turning of the wall, and the tower which lieth out from the king's high house, that was by the court of the prison. After him Pedaiah the son of Parosh.

26 Moreover the Nethinims dwelt in Ophel, unto the place over against the water gate toward the east, and the tower that lieth out.

27 After them the Tekoites repaired another piece, over against the great tower that lieth out, even unto the wall of Ophel.

28 From above the horse gate repaired the priests, every one over against his house.

29 After them repaired Zadok the son of Immer over against his house. After him repaired also Shemaiah the son of Shechaniah, the keeper of the east gate.

30 After him repaired Hananiah the son of Shelemiah, and Hanun the sixth son of Zalaph, another piece. After him repaired Meshullam the son of Berechiah over against his chamber.

31 After him repaired Malchiah the goldsmith's son unto the place of the Nethinims, and of the merchants, over against the gate Miphkad, and to the going up of the corner.

32 And between the going up of the corner unto the sheep gate repaired the goldsmiths and the merchants.

SHEEP GATE

TOWER OF MEAH

TOWER OF HANANEEL

After visiting the city with Ashur, let us now see if we can trace the city which he helped to rebuild. This is a challenging and complex task. But in the words of the Dutch explorer Jan Simons, *Jerusalem in the Old Testament* (Leiden, Brill, 1953):

> That it is at all possible, we owe much less to other authors and person-alities in and outside the Old Testament than to Nehemiah, who after a terrible disaster gave this city a new span of life.
> (p.458)

Today, some twenty-five centuries after Simons wrote his record, we can, by combining the richness of detail Nehemiah provides with the archaeo-logical data, walk the walls of Jerusalem in his company.

At first glance, the archaeological data may appear thin on the ground. In fact, if we look care-fully, scattered remains of the entire circumvallation can be detected.

Going verse by verse, we begin with Nehemiah 3:1:

THE SHEEP GATE

The Sheep Gate is the first feature men-tioned and also the last in Nehemiah's list of restored wall sections and gates. This gate was not referred to previously in the Old Testament record, whereas the next two features mentioned by Nehemiah, the Towers of Meah and Hananeel, were.

The Mishnah, a collection of rabbini-cal writings detailing the workings of the Temple and Jewish ritual and compiled in the second century A.D., records in its enumeration of the gates of the Temple Mount "the Tadi Gate" on the north, which was "not used at all." *Middot* 1:9 tells us that this gate had an under-ground passage which led to a chamber of immersion where priests went to pu-rify themselves. Furthermore, *Middot* 2:3 records that, unusually, among the gates

"Then Eliashib the high priest rose up with his brethren the priests, and they builded the Sheep Gate; they sanctified it, and set up the doors of it; even unto the Tower of Meah they sanctified it, unto the Tower of Hananeel" (Neh. 3:1).

(overleaf) Map of the archaeological remains from the city of Nehemiah. The name of the excavator/discoverer and the date of discovery are indicated in parentheses.

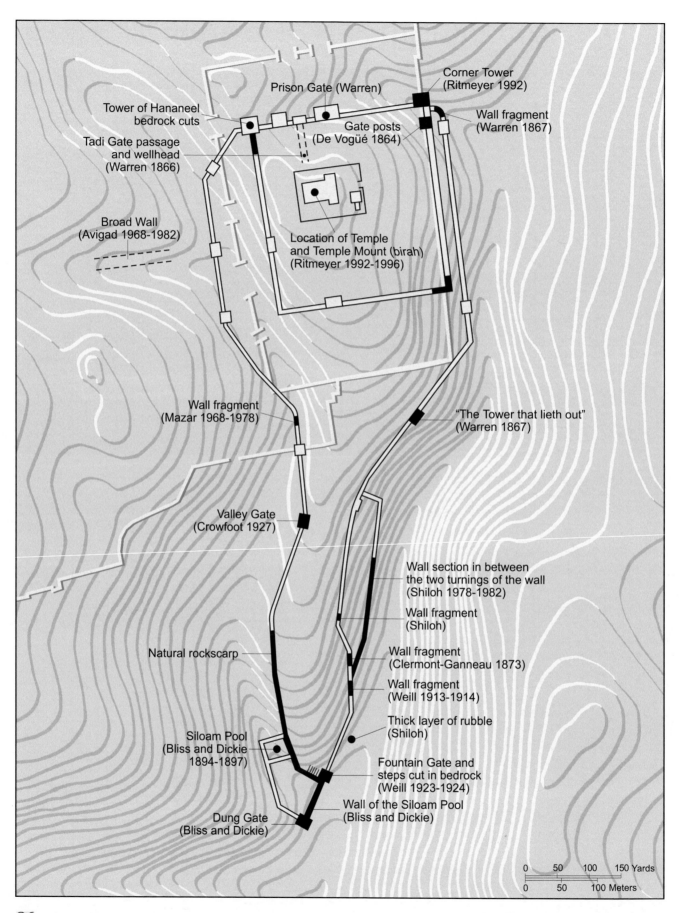

Corner Tower
(Ritmeyer 1992)

Prison Gate (Warren)

Tower of Hananeel
bedrock cuts

Wall fragment
(Warren 1867)

Gate posts
(De Vogüé 1864)

Tadi Gate passage
and wellhead
(Warren 1866)

Location of Temple
and Temple Mount (birah)
(Ritmeyer 1992-1996)

Broad Wall
(Avigad 1968-1982)

Wall fragment
(Mazar 1968-1978)

"The Tower that lieth out"
(Warren 1867)

Valley Gate
(Crowfoot 1927)

Wall section in between
the two turnings of the wall
(Shiloh 1978-1982)

Wall fragment
(Shiloh)

Natural rockscarp

Wall fragment
(Clermont-Ganneau 1873)

Wall fragment
(Weill 1913-1914)

Thick layer of rubble
(Shiloh)

Siloam Pool
(Bliss and Dickie
1894-1897)

Fountain Gate and
steps cut in bedrock
(Weill 1923-1924)

Wall of the Siloam Pool
(Bliss and Dickie)

Dung Gate
(Bliss and Dickie)

0   50   100   150 Yards

0   50   100 Meters

The only indication above ground of the Tadi Gate today is the well head of Cistern 1 which was photographed by the Russian photographer Narinsky in the nineteenth century (left). Here we see boys drawing water to fill their water-skins through this well head. This cistern is a precious piece of archaeological evidence—as we go on to follow the route of the wall, we will see just how precious!

of the Temple Mount, which had lintels, this gate had a pointed arch formed by two stones leaning against each other.

Sir Charles Warren, the great nineteenth-century explorer of Jerusalem, surveyed all the underground cisterns of the Temple Mount and identified his Cistern 1 with the Tadi Gate of *Middot*. It would appear that this structure, located in the northern wall of the raised platform, was originally built as an underground passageway and later plastered over and converted into a cistern. Its shape is most unlike a custom-built cistern, being long (130 ft./39.50 m) and narrow (only 24 ft./7.30 m). Its floor is located 30 feet (9.10 m) below the present-day surface of the Temple platform. The side walls of the passageway are cut out of the bedrock and the roofing is made of stone vaulting. At its northern end, the passageway is closed with a rough stone wall and from the appearance of a rubble wall at its southern terminus, it looks like it may have originally extended farther to the south. We know that when Herod the Great built his temple in the first century A.D., he extended the existing Temple platform to the north, east and west. When the extension to the north was made, the gate that stood at the end

of this passageway would have been buried and so disused, as indicated by *Middot* 1.3.

But can we identify this Tadi Gate as the Sheep Gate of Nehemiah? We know that the gates mentioned after this were in the northern wall (see below) and the mention of another gate to the east of it, the Prison Gate in Nehemiah 12:39, would give a probable location of the highest point in the north wall for the Sheep Gate. This is exactly where the passageway identified as the Tadi Gate is located.

(above) The cistern as seen today.

The tower of Hippicus from the time of Herod the Great in the Citadel, reminiscent of the Towers of Meah and Hananeel mentioned in Nehemiah 3:1.

There is another link, this time linguistic, between the Sheep Gate and the Tadi Gate. The meaning of the word "Tadi" remains unknown, but Professor Asher Kaufman suggests that the Hebrew letter *Daleth* can be interchanged with the letter *Lamed* (see Asher Kaufman, *The Temple Mount, Where is the Holy of Holies?*, Ha-Yera'eh Press, Jerusalem 2004, pp. 115–116). Thus Tadi could read Tali or Taleh, which means "lamb." He deduces from this that the Tadi Gate and the Sheep Gate were synonymous and that this gate was connected with the Lamb Chamber, thought to have stood on the north side of the Temple.

Why did Eliashib build this feature with his fellow priests? We have heard it suggested that this was a soft option for this team. Not so! On the contrary, this area was crucially important for the defense of the Temple Mount. The mount was surrounded by steep valleys on every side, except on the north. This was the reason why there had to be defensive towers on the north. And it was incumbent upon Eliashib as the appointed leader of the nation to take the lead in fortifying this vulnerable location. We are not sure whether the gate protruded from the wall or not, but we can be sure, from verse 3 where it is recorded that Eliashib laid the beams, set up the doors, locks and bars, that it was a well-fortified gate after he finished with it. The use of the word "sanctified" here: "they sanctified it . . . they sanctified it unto the Tower of Hananeel," is unique among the descriptions of buildings or repairing the wall and probably refers to the holiness expected from the priests: "Thou shalt sanctify him therefore; for he offereth the bread of thy God; he shall be holy unto thee: for I the LORD, which sanctify you, am holy" (Lev. 21: 1–15). It must be a confirmation of how important it was that the High Priest set the example by commencing at this particular spot in preference to his own house (cf. vs. 20–21).

THE TOWER OF MEAH

Although there is no prior or later reference to the Tower of Meah (= Hundred) in Scripture, its position is fixed by the record as being between the Sheep Gate and the Tower of Hananeel. As we shall see in the next section, the Tower of Hananeel must be near the northwest corner of the Temple Mount of that time.

No archaeological remains of the Tower of Meah are extant, but Simons (p. 429, n.2) has a most interesting suggestion that this tower was, in fact, the eastern tower of a fortress located at this corner of the pre-exilic Temple Mount, of which Hananeel was the western. What the hundred referred to in the name of this tower is unknown. The number 100 usually signifies completeness, but did it refer to mighty men, measurements or something else entirely?

THE TOWER OF HANANEEL

Much more can be said about the Tower of Hananeel as it is well attested in Scripture. It is given as one of the city's four extreme points in the prophecy of Zechariah 14:10 and obviously referred to as the most northerly point in the city wall. It is referred to similarly when describing how the city will be built up in the future age in Jeremiah 31:38. These prophecies, although they described the ideal envisioned by the prophet, used features familiar to the Israelites at the end of the First Temple period.

In the Book of Nehemiah, the Tower of Meah is always mentioned together with the Tower of Hananeel and, as already stated, it seems logical to assume that they were the twin towers of a defensive fortress situated at the northwestern corner of the Temple Mount of the period. They were, of course destroyed in the Babylonian invasion of Jerusalem and here the text indicates rebuilding.

Now to archaeological evidence for

this tower. Just to the north of the stairway leading up to the Muslim platform at its northwestern corner are bedrock cuts. The bedrock has been cut at right angles and parallel to the northern wall of the square Temple Mount. These bedrock remains may have formed the foundation for the Tower of Hananeel. The fact that the towers must have been located where we show them in the model is confirmed by later historical sources. According to Josephus:

At an angle on the north side, there had been built a citadel well fortified and of unusual strength. It was the kings and high priests of the Asamonaean (Hasmonean) family before Herod who had built it and called it "baris." (Ant. 15.403)

And then when Herod the Great extended the Temple platform across the ditch that separated it from the high hill, Josephus described the Antonia Fortress that he built "at the angle where two porticoes, the western and the northern, of the first court of the Temple met; it was built upon a rock fifty cubits high and on all sides precipitous" (*War* 5.238). Although the fortress had moved, it still stood in the same place vis-a-vis the Temple platform, i.e. on the dangerous ridge north of the Temple hill, acting as a guardian to the Temple. So, the most compelling evidence for the location of these two towers is that they were needed here, as were their successors!

THE WALL IN BETWEEN (Neh. 3:2)

This verse records the men of Jericho building next to Zaccur, son of Imri. Although there is no archaeological evidence for this stretch of wall, the topography here dictates a turning in the wall. The lay of the land between the Tower of Hananeel and the Central Valley

(1) "And next unto him builded the men of Jericho. (2) And next to them builded Zaccur the son of Imri." (Neh. 3:2)

(see illustration on previous page) means that two teams would have better effected the work involved, with each building half a section. Their wall sections had to be integrated with one another and also had to be bonded in the towers, as vertical seams would weaken the wall. What an exercise in collaboration, with the phrase "and next to him builded," setting a wonderful pattern of how this work was to be accomplished in fifty-two days! Here we must bear in mind that the wall built was wide enough for the procession described in Nehemiah 12:37–39 to walk over. Judging from the ramparts above the present-day Old City walls of Jerusalem and of York in the United Kingdom, we know that the width of these walls must be at least 6.5 feet (2 m) for walking comfortably.

"But the fish gate did the sons of Hassenaah build, who also laid the beams thereof, and set up the doors thereof, the locks thereof, and the bars thereof." (Neh. 3:3)

THE FISH GATE (Neh. 3:3)

The Fish Gate is also mentioned in the circuit of the walls in Nehemiah 12:39, where it is located in exactly the same place between the Tower of Hananeel and the Old Gate, but in reverse order, as the circuit goes in the opposite direction to the description of the building of the wall sections. There are also references to this gate in 2 Chronicles 33:14, where it is included in the wall built by King Manasseh and in Zephaniah 1:10–11, which mentions it as one of the few places in Jerusalem which felt the divine wrath when the Babylonians came. The mention of the Fish Gate in Zephaniah indicates that the Babylonians attacked the city from the northwest. From the latter verse, we may understand that it was located close to the Mishneh (English—"the Second") Quarter, which was located on the Western Hill, surrounded by Hezekiah's wall—extolled by the psalmist when describing Jerusalem in Psalm 122 as "a city which is compact (joined) together." The blue line shown on the model does not indicate a river, but the dry riverbed of the Central Valley (later called the Tyropoeon or Cheesemakers Valley by Josephus). The location of the Fish Gate opening onto this valley gave it a strategic position

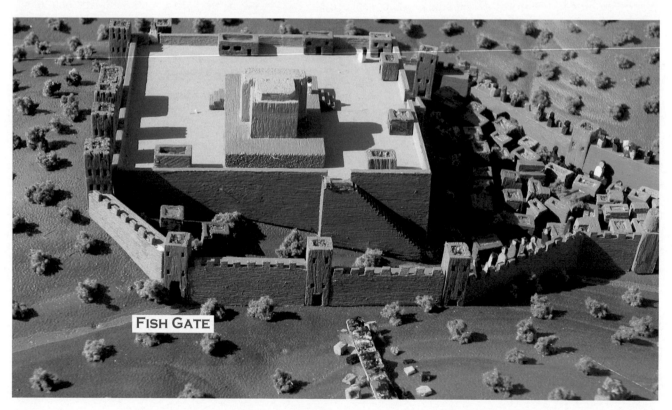

FISH GATE

and one of considerable commercial value, as the road which bypassed it ran all the way to Joppa. It must have been through here that the merchants of Tyre, who appeared to have the monopoly on selling fish, brought their wares on the Sabbath day, only to be berated by Nehemiah (Neh.13:15). Outside this gate, also, we may picture the group of merchants bedded down for the night, waiting for the opening of the gates on the morning of the Sabbath until Nehemiah's wrath definitively put an end to trading on the holy day.

Another point to consider is that from the Sheep Gate up to this point, the record speaks of building, whereas from here on, the word "repairing" is used.

It would appear that when Nebuchadnezzar had "brake down the walls of Jerusalem round about" (2 Kgs 25:9), he must have actually destroyed this most vulnerable of wall sections on the northern ridge from which point he took the Temple Mount. The task of rebuilding this latter area from scratch must have been truly prodigious! And of course, it was not only masonry work that was involved. Nehemiah had asked for: "beams for the gates of the palace which appertained to the house and for the walls of the city and for the house that I shall enter into" (2:8). As with all the entrances mentioned in Nehemiah's wall, we must envision massive gates with heavy "locks and bars."

"And it came to pass, that when the gates of Jerusalem began to be dark before the sabbath, I commanded that the gates should be shut, and charged that they should not be opened till after the sabbath.... So the merchants and sellers of all kind of ware lodged without Jerusalem once or twice." (Neh. 13:19–20)

FISH GATE

1 2 3 4 5 6 7

OLD GATE

THE BROAD WALL

THE WALL IN BETWEEN (Neh. 3:4–5)

In this section of wall, four teams worked side by side repairing the walls that were broken down and learning the invaluable skills of cooperation. The fourth group mentioned here, the Tekoites, were at a disadvantage, as their nobles thought the work of building beneath them. However, as we shall see later, nobles from other towns joined in the work wholeheartedly.

THE OLD GATE (Neh. 3:6)

The Old Gate was probably called by this name, as it may have been part of the Broad Wall built by King Hezekiah (of which more later) and needed to be adapted in order to incorporate it into the new wall of Nehemiah. This gate is located just in front of the Broad Wall

of which it may have been part. The direction of the gate opening would most likely have had to be changed, because, as can be seen in our model, the opening would have had to face west, whereas when it was a gate in the Broad Wall, the opening would have faced north.

THE WALL IN BETWEEN (Neh. 3:7–8)

The section referred to in Nehemiah 3: 7 appears to have terminated opposite a notable building which was a handy reference point among the smaller buildings of the city.

The two sections mentioned in Nehemiah 3:8 were constructed by men whose work was usually of a delicate and refined nature, which shows the extraordinary willingness of spirit that was prevalent in Jerusalem at that time.

With the Broad Wall, we are again on archaeological terra firma. The finding of this wall was one of the highlights of the Jewish Quarter excavations led by Nahman Avigad from 1968 to 1982. Prior to its discovery, the "minimalist" position, which held that the Western Hill was not settled in the Israelite period, held sway.

However, the wall found by Avigad's team was, judging by its thickness and height, clearly a city wall and was found running west from the Temple Mount towards the northwestern corner of the Western Hill. The continuous stretch of wall was 23 feet (7 m) broad and in places stood to seven courses of stones. Its dating to the Israelite period was never in doubt, as pottery consistent with Iron Age II was found along the entire base of the wall. When placed on a topographical map of Jerusalem, it provided clear evidence that a new quarter, probably the Mishneh of 2 Kings 22: 14 and 2 Chronicles 34:22, had been enclosed by a new city wall during this period. The most logical conclusion is that the new quarter was built to accommodate the influx of refugees from the Assyrian invasion in the eighth century B.C.

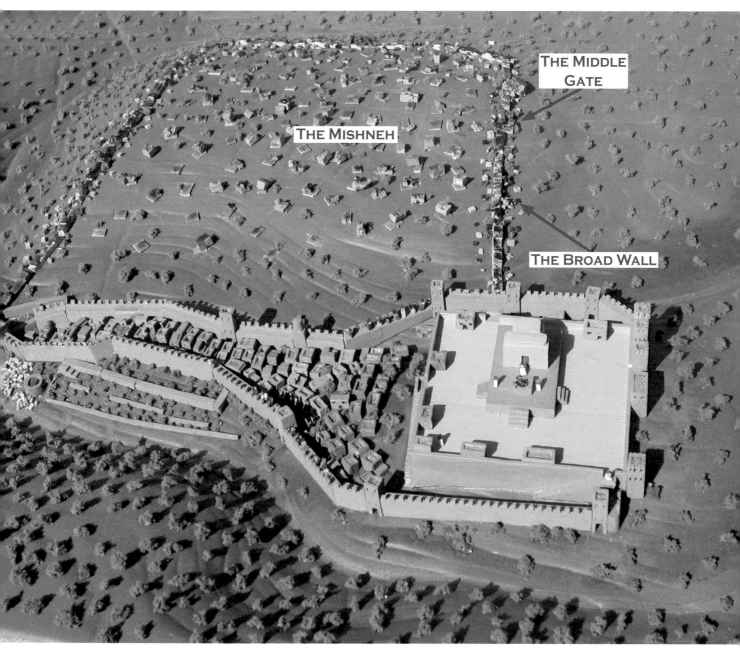

THE MIDDLE GATE

THE MISHNEH

THE BROAD WALL

On the model, a gate is shown in the northern wall of the ruined Mishneh. In the area of the gate, the Broad Wall ran a little to the south, circumventing a small valley located in this area. Sometime after the time of Hezekiah, the line of the wall was straightened out and a gate built on foundations laid deep across the valley. Thsi gate has been identified with the Middle Gate mentioned in Jeremiah 39:3, where the Babylonian princes sat following the conquest of the city by Nebuchadnezzar in 586 B.C.

It is clear from the paucity of finds from the Persian period on the Western Hill that this area was unoccupied during this period. Thus, the formidable Broad Wall, the Mishneh quarter and the Middle Gate, all lay outside the area repaired by Nehemiah, but the ruins of this quarter would have been a notable feature of the city of the faithful builder. For us, the mention of the Broad Wall along this section of Nehemiah's wall serves to confirm the truth of the record!

Model of Nehemiah's Jerusalem, looking west.

Reconstruction of the Middle Gate (left) and the excavated remains (below) located in today's Jewish Quarter of the Old City.

(above) Remains of the Broad Wall, built over a house from an earlier period. While digging, poignant evidence was found of the verse in Isaiah 22:10, describing the building of the Broad Wall in preparation for the Assyrian invasion: "Ye have numbered the houses of Jerusalem and the houses have ye broken down to fortify the wall." It would appear that King Hezekiah's workmen had counted the houses that would obstruct the planned wall and marked them for destruction. Next to the thick wall, the corner of an Israelite house was revealed. The remaining stones were re-used in the mighty fortification, meaning that some of Jerusalem's inhabitants, probably the most vulnerable, were dispossessed.

GATE OF EPHRAIM

THE GATE OF EPHRAIM (Neh. 12:38–40)

In the model, we have inserted the Gate of Ephraim in between the Old Gate and the Tower of the Furnaces, even though there is no mention of such a gate in Nehemiah 3. However, when the wall was completed and we follow the route of the dedicatory company that walked over the wall on the western side of the city, we find it mentioned in Nehemiah 12. Here, the company encounter the Gate of Ephraim after the Tower of the Furnaces and before the Old Gate (Neh. 12:38–39). The relatively high ground in this area would also be an appropriate place to build a gate, as from that point on the wall descended into the Tyropoeon Valley.

THE WALL IN BETWEEN AND THE TOWER OF FURNACES (Neh. 3:9–12)

Here is the first instance where one of the builders is actually building the wall opposite his own house, which would have laid inside the walls. What a tremendously motivating factor that would have been for Jedaiah, who would have looked to the protection that the wall would have afforded his family!

This section, from the Ephraim Gate down into the Valley (note how the wall crosses over the riverbed) was built by Rephaiah and Jedaiah. It is logical that they would have divided this section between them. Jedaiah's house was probably in the City of David and, according to the topography at this point, the wall turned due south. The beginning of this southern stretch would have been

"And the other company of them that gave thanks went over against them, and I after them, and the half of the people upon the wall, from beyond the tower of the furnaces even unto the broad wall; And from above the gate of Ephraim, and above the old gate, and above the fish gate, and the tower of Hananeel, and the tower of Meah, even unto the sheep gate: and they stood still in the prison gate. So stood the two companies of them that gave thanks in the house of God, and I, and the half of the rulers with me."

(Neh. 12:38–40)

built by Hattush. A fragment of wall that may correspond to this section was excavated deep in the Tyropoeon Valley during the Temple Mount excavations led by Prof. Benjamin Mazar from 1968 to 1978. Presently it lies beneath the largest Umayyad palace south of the Temple Mount.

Malchijah would have continued the stretch of wall begun by Hattush. His work was continued by Hashub who also built the Tower of the Furnaces. A typical section would have been about 82 feet (25 m) long.

The Tower of the Furnaces (Migdal haTannurim) may have been so called because of its proximity to the Bakers' Street mentioned in Jeremiah 37:21. In the model, it is represented by a tower surmounted by a chimney (no. 5).

Up to this point, the wall sections built by the different builders were more or less equal, but looking at the model, we find that Shallum and his daughters (Neh. 3:12) built an unusually long section (about 82 yds./75 m), about three times as long as other sections built by individuals. It is possible that the wall here was preserved to a substantial height as were the remains of the Valley Gate, which we will discuss next. As the builders always endeavored to build on top of the old foundations, this would have been a considerable help to the father-and-daughters team.

THE VALLEY GATE (Neh. 3:13)

The Valley Gate is another element of Nehemiah's wall for which we have archaeological evidence. In 1927, J. W. Crowfoot discovered in this area a stretch of wall into which was built a 20-foot (6-m) high gate of very large stones which gave access to the City of

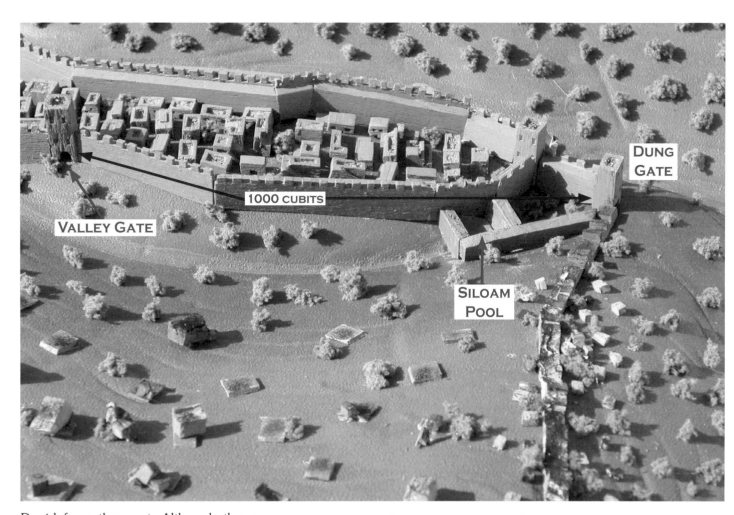

VALLEY GATE

1000 CUBITS

SILOAM POOL

DUNG GATE

David from the west. Although the gate was used by the Hasmoneans, as witnessed by the hoard of Maccabean coins found in the gateway, the lower courses appear to date back some centuries earlier, making it a prime candidate for the Valley Gate of Nehemiah 3. The 1,000-cubit (525-m) length wall referred to here has been questioned by some. However, an examination of the local topography helps to put this construction feat into perspective. The builders were constructing on top of a high rock scarp, so only a low wall was required. If others had to build a 15-foot (4.5-m) high wall, the latter team would only have had to build 3 feet (1 m) in order to protect the defenders of the city. Here again is a wonderful confirmation of the veracity of Nehemiah's account.

(above) "The valley gate repaired Hanun, and the inhabitants of Zanoah; they built it, and set up the doors thereof, the locks thereof, and the bars thereof, and a thousand cubits on the wall unto the dung gate." (Neh. 3:13)

(left) The "Valley Gate" discovered by J. W. Crowfoot in 1927.

KING'S GARDEN

DUNG GATE

"But the dung gate repaired Malchiah the son of Rechab, the ruler of part of Beth-haccerem; he built it, and set up the doors thereof, the locks thereof, and the bars thereof." (Neh. 3:14)

(right) A sketch of the Dung Gate and the Pool of Siloam to its north, from Bliss and Dickie's Excavations at Jerusalem, *1894–97.*

THE DUNG GATE (Neh. 3:14)

Archaeologists have not found the Dung Gate (*Sha'ar Ashpot*) of Nehemiah, but relevant remains have been found in the area in which, according to the Book of Nehemiah, the gate must have been located. Frederick Bliss and Archibald Dickie excavated here at the Siloam Pool from 1894 to 1897 and discovered a gate which, from its masonry, appears to be a Hellenistic rebuild of an earlier gateway. The Dung Gate would have been used to take out all the city's rubbish to the Hinnom Valley.

THE FOUNTAIN GATE AND POOL OF SILOAM (Neh. 3:15)

The Fountain Gate appears to have been named after the nearby spring of En-rogel, which was known to Nehemiah as the Dragon Well (Neh. 2:13). While the Dung Gate gave access to the rubbish tips of the Hinnom Valley, the Fountain Gate was used more to enter and exit the city from the Kidron Valley and to gain access to water. The Dung Gate was closer to the Hinnom Valley and originally gave access to the city of

"But the gate of the fountain repaired Shallun the son of Colhozeh, the ruler of part of Mizpah; he built it, and covered it, and set up the doors thereof, the locks thereof, and the bars thereof, and the wall of the pool of Siloah by the king's garden, and unto the stairs that go down from the city of David."

(Neh. 3:15)

DUNG GATE

FOUNTAIN GATE

We do not know what the Siloam Pool looked like in the Persian period, but the description of the work of Hezekiah: "Ye made also a ditch between the two walls for the water of the old pool," firmly places it between the old city wall, which Nehemiah repaired and the new wall built by Hezekiah to encompass the Western Hill.
As today a steep rockscarp forms the eastern boundary of the Siloam Pool, we suggest in the model that an enclosing wall was built to form a kind of reservoir. Its southern wall probably also bordered the King's Garden. Excavations at the Siloam Pool by Bliss and Dickie, and later excavators, have yielded only Herodian (some say Roman) remains. Recent excavations revealed the beginning of a stepped pool, but it is too early to say if this was the original Siloam Pool.

Hezekiah from the south, whereas the Fountain Gate allowed entry to the city proper from the east. From the text, the Fountain Gate is obviously close to the King's Garden and is connected with the wall of the Pool of Siloam, which is a place where the two city walls met. The people of the time apparently believed the Siloam Pool to be a fountain and did not know that the water came from the Gihon Spring.

In 1923–24 the French archaeologist Raymond Weill conducted excavations in this area. He found that the bedrock had been transformed into a vertical wall of c. 26 feet (8 m) high in order to enhance the defences in the southern part of the city. In this scarp he found a 10-foot (3-m) wide opening, which he identified as the Fountain Gate.

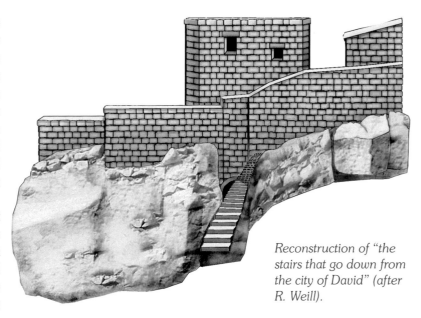

Reconstruction of "the stairs that go down from the city of David" (after R. Weill).

THE KING'S GARDEN

One cannot join the Western Hill of Jerusalem to the Eastern Hill (as Hezekiah did) without closing the mouth of the Tyropoeon with a massive wall. For this wall, which is here called "the wall of the Pool of Siloah," we again have archaeological evidence. The British team of excavators, Frederick Bliss and Archibald Dickie, sank a series of tunnels across the valley bed and found evidence for a wide dam reinforced with pilasters. The most likely location for the King's Garden would have been inside this wall. With this kind of construction, it would also have been protected by the continuation of the western border of the Siloam Pool.

THE STAIRS THAT GO DOWN FROM THE CITY OF DAVID

The topography of the southern end of the City of David is so steep that it demands the inclusion of a staircase for ease of descent to the Fountain Gate. The path of the "stairs that go down from the city of David" is still today the way one descends from the eastern ridge. In his excavations in this area,

Raymond Weill discovered a 36-foot (11-m) high staircase going through the gap in the rockscarp, which he had identified, as mentioned earlier, as the Fountain Gate.

Shallum, the son of Col-hozeh, repaired the Fountain Gate, the wall of the Pool of Siloam to the stairs of the City of David. This was a very steep area and a critical point at the southernmost tip of the city. All these combined to form the city's southern defense system, thus it made sense to put one leader in charge of this section in its entirety.

THE SEPULCHRES OF DAVID (Neh. 3:16)

We have not indicated the location of the Sepulchres of David, but they must be slightly north of the Fountain Gate. In excavations carried out by Raymond Weill in 1913–14, on the eastern slope of the Eastern Hill, he found two man-made tombs which he identified as those of the Royal House of David. However, as the tomb was robbed of its contents in the Roman period, we cannot, with any certainty, attribute this tomb to the time of the kings and the site remains an archaeological mystery. One thing is certain, the tombs represented Jerusalem for Nehemiah, as he said to the

The King's Garden
would probably date to
the time of Solomon,
who recorded in the
Book of Ecclesiastes 2:5:
"I planted me gardens
and orchards, and I
planted trees in them
of all kind of fruits." It
would also correspond
to the description of the
bride in the Song of
Songs 4:12: "A garden
inclosed is my sister, my
spouse; a spring shut
up, a fountain sealed."
In this area today (right),
figs and pomegranates
still flourish because of
the abundance of water.

Tombs found on the Eastern Hill which the French archaeologist Raymond Weill identified as those of the House of David.

Persian king in Shushan: "why should not my countenance be sad, when the city, the place of my father's sepulchres lieth waste..." (Neh. 2:3). By the way, it is here at this point that Nehemiah be-

gins to describe most of the remaining repaired sections by means of nearby reference points, such as the sepulchres of David.

Reconstruction of Tombs T1 and T2 excavated by R. Weill. One of these, T1, is particularly well preserved and consists of a vaulted tunnel, 52.5 feet (16 m) long, 8 feet (2.5 m) wide, indicating that it had obviously been used as a tomb. However, as the site was used as a quarry in the Roman period and robbed of its contents, there is still no definitive proof of the structure's use or date.

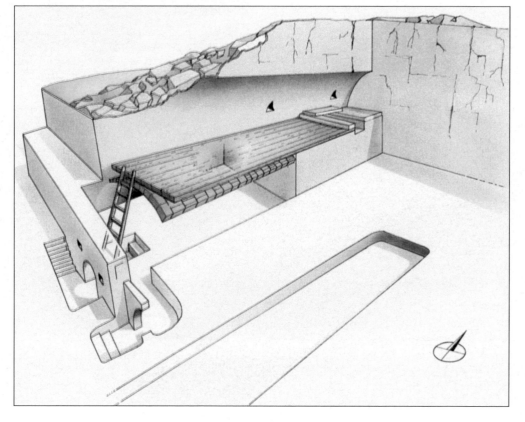

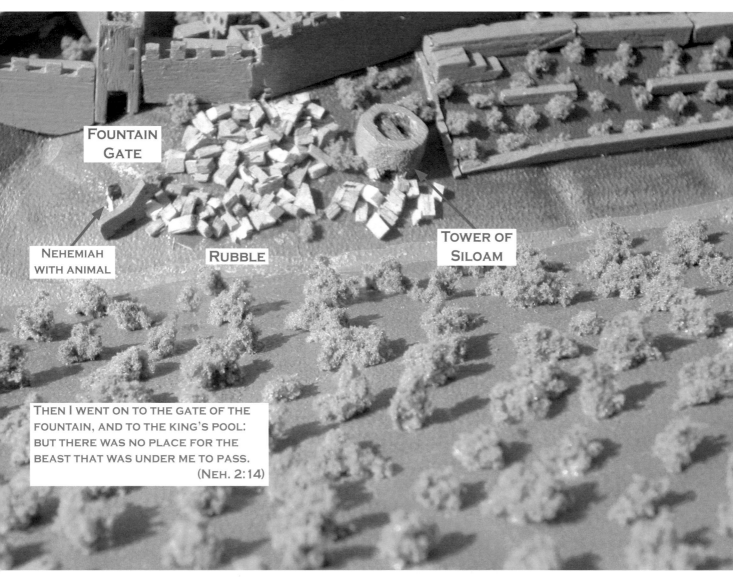

FOUNTAIN
GATE

NEHEMIAH
WITH ANIMAL

RUBBLE

TOWER OF
SILOAM

THEN I WENT ON TO THE GATE OF THE
FOUNTAIN, AND TO THE KING'S POOL:
BUT THERE WAS NO PLACE FOR THE
BEAST THAT WAS UNDER ME TO PASS.
(NEH. 2:14)

At the very top left of this picture (above), the city wall built by Nehemiah is visible. At the bottom of the picture, we see the Israelite houses which were destroyed by the Babylonians. Overlaying this and highlighted, is the thick layer of rubble of the houses that were built higher up the slope. (above right) A close-up view.

At this point in the model, we have inserted a pile of rubble, the existence of which is implied in the chapter on Nehemiah's night journey. Archaeological evidence for this was discovered by Yigal Shiloh in his Stratum 9 of Area D1 of the City of David excavations. A thick layer of tumbled debris was found on the surface of the slope. It is quite easy to imagine this as being a serious obstacle for the donkey carrying Nehemiah.

(1) "After him repaired Nehemiah the son of Azbuk, the ruler of the half part of Beth-zur, unto the place over against the sepulchres of David, and to the pool that was made, and unto the house of the mighty.
(2) "After him repaired the Levites, Rehum the son of Bani.
(3) "Next unto him repaired Hashabiah, the ruler of the half part of Keilah, in his part.
(4) "After him repaired their brethren, Bavai the son of Henadad, the ruler of the half part of Keilah.
(5) "And next to him repaired Ezer the son of Jeshua, the ruler of Mizpah, another piece over against the going up to the armoury at the turning of the wall."
(Neh. 3:16–19)

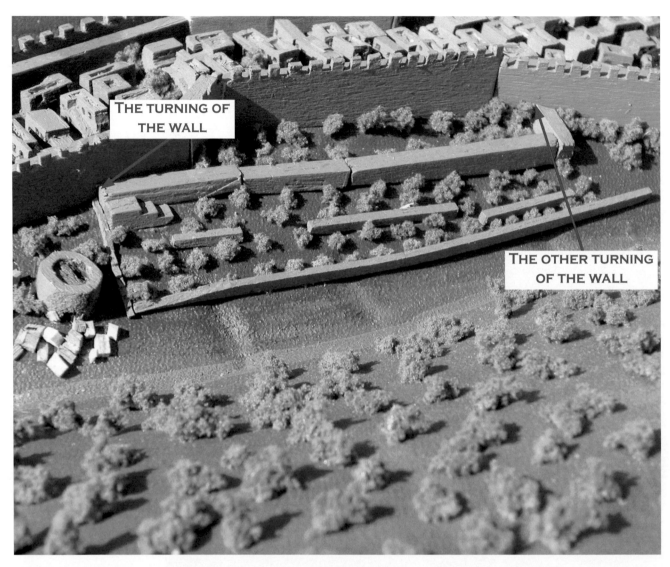

THE TURNING OF
THE WALL

THE OTHER TURNING
OF THE WALL

This illustration shows clearly how the old city wall was left out and used as an agricultural terrace wall. From the point where you can see Nehemiah's wall, the old wall used to turn and go down, but Nehemiah left the old Canaanite city wall out. The point where this happens is called the "turning of the wall."

THE POOL THAT WAS MADE

This pool is somewhat of an enigma and is not depicted on the model. It may be synonymous with the "king's pool" mentioned in the text of Nehemiah's night journey around the destroyed city in Nehemiah 2:14.

THE HOUSE OF THE MIGHTY

It is evident from references in the Bible concerning the monarchy that there were a group of mighty men who protected the king. A poetic reference to them is to be found in Song 3:7–8:

> *Behold his bed, which is Solomon's; threescore valiant men are about it, of the valiant of Israel.*
>
> *They all hold swords, being expert in*

war: every man hath his sword upon his thigh because of fear in the night.

In his area E1, Yigal Shiloh found a four-room building which he called "The Ashlar House." Although the layout of the so-called four-roomed house is well known from the Israelite period, this one is notable for the huge ashlars used in the construction of its corners. The house was also notable for its size, measuring 39×43 feet (12×13 m), which is larger than the usual four-roomed house and would indicate a public function. It was located inside the city wall of Jerusalem when the building was destroyed by the Babylonians in 586 B.C. When Nehemiah rebuilt the eastern wall of the city in this area, the

Ashlar House was left outside the wall. Although the house itself was not rebuilt, its remains were still an important landmark in the time of Nehemiah, being in a location higher than its surroundings. Just above the ashlar building is a rock-scarp, on top of which a short section of Nehemiah's city wall was uncovered.

THE ARMOURY AND THE TURNING OF THE WALL (Neh. 3:19)

Again the armoury cannot be identified, but it appears logical from the text that it was in close proximity to the "house of the mighty." It is probably synonymous with the "house of armour" that Hezekiah showed to the messengers from Babylon in Isaiah 39:2.

Now the "turning of the wall" mentioned in this verse is the first of two turnings in the wall in this chapter, the other being mentioned in verse 24. Thrillingly, a wall fragment dating from the Persian period and which runs a bit higher on the slope than the city wall of the previous period, necessitating a turning or a change in direction, was found in 1873 by the French excavator Charles Clermont-Ganneau. Later, the southern continuation of this section, which is still visible today (see above), was found by Weill. More recently, another section has been found by Shiloh. The city of Nehemiah was much smaller than the city just before the exile, not just because it left out the Western Hill. Restricted to the eastern ridge, it also did not include the steep eastern slope of the eastern hill.

The first "turning of the wall," first discovered by R. Weill, is visible to this day.

NEHEMIAH 3:20–24

"After him Baruch the son of Zabbai earnestly repaired the other piece, from the turning of the wall unto the door of the house of Eliashib the high priest.

After him repaired Meremoth the son of Urijah the son of Koz another piece, from the door of the house of Eliashib even to the end of the house of Eliashib

And after him repaired the priests, the men of the plain.

After him repaired Benjamin and Hashub over against their house.

After him repaired Azariah the son of Maaseiah the son of Ananiah by his house.

After him repaired Binnui the son of Henadad another piece, from the house of Azariah unto the turning of the wall, even unto the corner."

(Neh. 3:20–24)

NEHEMIAH 3:20–24

Giving the reference, "from the door of the house of Eliashib even to the end of the house of Eliashib" (Neh. 3:21), would imply that the high priest had a fairly sizable dwelling and, of course, he was busy building the Sheep Gate on the northern wall! Meremoth must have been a very diligent worker, as he had already built the first section of the city wall next to the Fish Gate.

As mentioned above, evidence of

Nehemiah's wall has also been found in the area excavated by Yigal Shiloh, designated E1. The second turning referred to in verse 24 must be located north of Shiloh's Area G. Because of the steepness of the slope of the Kidron Valley, it is most likely that somewhere north of Area G, the city wall would have gone straight up the steep slope to join with the great "tower which lieth out." This point would constitute the second "turning of the wall."

NEHEMIAH 3:25

"Palal the son of Uzai, over against the turning of the wall, and the tower which lieth out from the king's high house, that was by the court of the prison. After him Pedaiah the son of Parosh." (Neh. 3:25)

THE TOWER WHICH LIETH OUT (Neh. 3:25)

A fortification which could be identified as "the tower which lieth out" was found by Charles Warren in 1867–70 (see below under the Ophel).

THE KING'S HIGH HOUSE

This is enigmatic. It may have something to do with the House of Millo where King Joash was murdered (2 Kgs 12:20).

THE COURT OF THE PRISON

The Prison may have been part of the King's House. In Jeremiah 38, the Court of the Prison, where Jeremiah was cast into a dungeon by the princes of his day, is described as being under the treasury of the house of the king (vs. 11).

THE NETHINIMS AND THE OPHEL (Neh. 3:26–27)

The term "Nethinim" derives from the Hebrew root "*nathan*" which means "to give" and refers to those who were especially dedicated to the Temple services. Originally, the Levites were called by this term in Numbers 8:14–16:

Thus shalt thou separate the Levites from among the children of Israel: and

OPHEL

WATER GATE

HORSE GATE

the Levites shall be mine.

And after that shall the Levites go in to do the service of the tabernacle of the congregation: and thou shalt cleanse them, and offer them for an offering.

For they are wholly given (nethunim, nethunim—a derivative of nethinim) unto me from among the children of Israel; instead of such as open every womb, even instead of the firstborn of all the children of Israel, have I taken them unto me.

Later on, others, including Gentiles, were allowed to help the Levites with the service and appropriated the name "Nethinims." A large number of Nethinims had returned from Babylon and,

as we are told in Nehemiah 7:73, lived in "their cities," but those who lived in Jerusalem were to be found near the Water Gate, which would point to their being employed as drawers of water.

The precise location of the Ophel used to be one of the perennial questions of the archaeology of Jerusalem. However, since the excavations of the Temple Mount, it is clear that the high area south of the Temple Mount is the Ophel. The Hebrew root from which "Ophel" is derived signifies "to rise up" or "to swell." Bible translators have translated it as "tower" or "citadel" or simply left it untranslated. It would appear to refer to that part of the city which was higher

"Moreover the Nethinims dwelt in Ophel, unto the place over against the water gate toward the east, and the tower that lieth out. After them the Tekoites repaired another piece, over against the great tower that lieth out, even unto the wall of Ophel."
(Neh. 3:26–27)

The excavated remains of the Ophel located south of the Temple Mount.

Another view of the Ophel, looking west toward the modern city of Jerusalem.

than the rest, an area that was fortified and included the royal palace. Out of this Jerusalem context, the word is simply translated as "fort" (Isa. 32:14).

This area was certainly well fortified and "the great tower that lieth out" found by Warren is only part of this fortification. In 1976, Prof. Benjamin Mazar had discovered a complex of Iron Age II buildings in the southeastern part of his excavations. He had identified them as the House of Millo (Beth Millo) of 2 Kings 12:21, where Joash was assassinated and which may be

the king's house referred to above. He again excavated the area in 1986–87 with Eilat Mazar and found a complex of building units which interconnected with those he had previously identified as the Beth Millo. The excavators subsequently identified this complex, with its Buildings C and D, as a four-chambered gatehouse typical of the Iron Age II type and claimed it as the Water Gate. This, of course, lay just inside "the great tower that lieth out" and would have been reached by an outer gateway, as yet undiscovered. The identification

The Wall of the Ophel would simply have been the wall that fortified the Ophel. A massive wall was found in the excavations near the southeastern corner. It had been the line for the city fortifications from the Iron Age up to the Byzantine period. The empress Eudocia, who in the fifth century rebuilt the city wall, was the last to build there. No remains from the time of Nehemiah have been identified, but the Iron Age wall was so well preserved that it would most likely have been used by Nehemiah. The construction work done by the Tekoites would not have been too arduous here because of the good state of preservation of the wall. In the center of the photograph, the outline of the tunnel constructed by Charles Warren during his explorations of this area can be seen.

of this complex of buildings with the Water Gate, as originally proposed by the author, is not one hundred percent sure however, as the building does appear to have had a strong connection with storage. About forty storage vessels were found in Building C, in what has since been identified as the gatehouse chamber. The adjoining Building D contained twelve pithoi or gigantic storage jars, used to store oil or wine and would definitely appear to have been used for storage.

The late Professor Nahman Avigad believed the complex to be an independent building, similar to one found in Samaria which dated to the ninth century B.C. and not a gatehouse. It would be fitting, however, if a gateway called "The Water Gate" had stood in this area, as a channel did lead into this area from the Pools of Bethesda. This channel can be seen on Warren's

drawings of the two towers (which later had to be revised). The author had conducted a dig across the road from these excavations in 1973, in order to find the top of these towers. Just before the top of Warren's Tower was reached, the excavations were stopped by Orthodox Jews who claimed that there were tombs in this area.

If this is truly the Water Gate, it would explain why these few verses in Nehemiah 3 are so interrelated. The "great tower which lieth out" fortified the Ophel, into which one entered by means of the Water Gate, soon reaching the "king's high house" in the separate royal quarter of the city. It should be noted that here, in contrast to the gates mentioned prior to verse 16, it is not explicitly said that the gate was repaired. In this case, the gate is simply used as a reference.

Sir Charles Warren's reconstruction of the two ashlar-built towers he discovered in the Ophel area during his excavations from 1867 to 1870. Note the channel ("drain") at the bottom of his drawing.

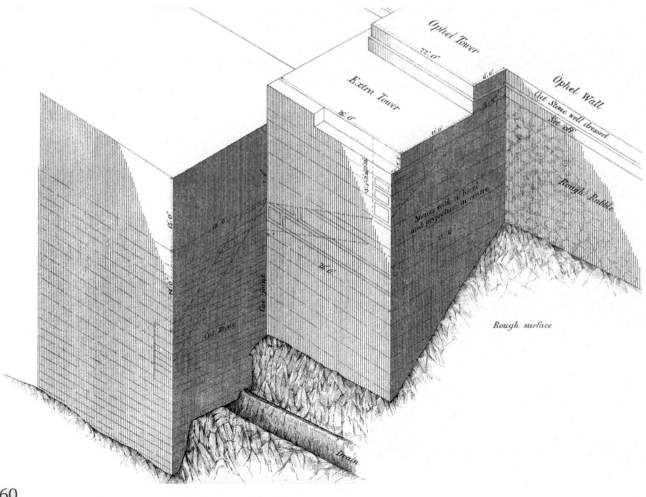

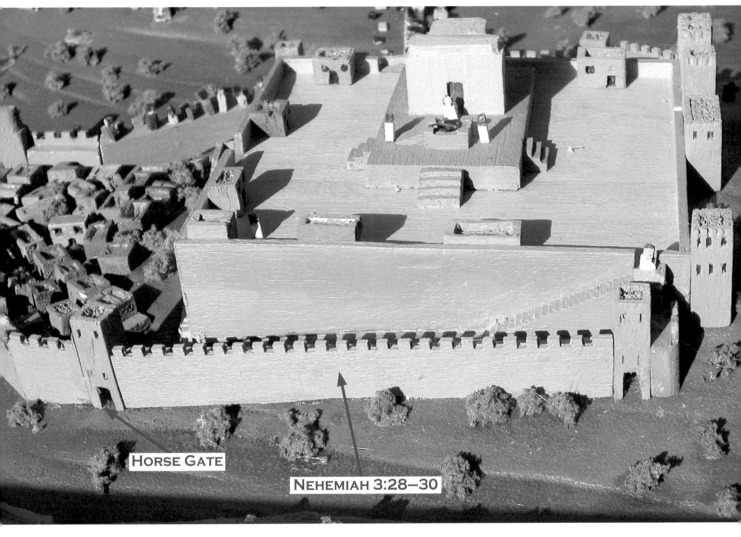

HORSE GATE

NEHEMIAH 3:28–30

THE HORSE GATE (Neh. 3: 28–30)

All we know about the Horse Gate is that it must have been located higher up than the area just previously described. Additionally, from 2 Chronicles 23: 15, which records Athaliah being slain "when she was come to the entering of the horse gate by the king's house," we can infer that the gate must have been near the king's house. Although we have no archaeological evidence, Nehemiah's mention of this gate as being located just here, has all the marks of accuracy. The fact that it was the priests who were building opposite their own houses in this area also has the hallmark of truth, as the Ophel was the place in

which many of the Jerusalem priests lived. Another connection is that the underground spaces at the southeastern corner of the present-day Temple Mount were called Solomon's Stables by the Crusaders, as they had assumed that the Horse Gate was in this area and that Solomon would have kept his horses there.

The participation of Meshullam in repairing the walls did not prevent him from associating with Tobiah the Ammonite, as his daughter later married the latter's son. Although it is not mentioned in the biblical text, it appears from the archaeological findings that the wall repaired by the persons mentioned here is actually a wall parallel to the eastern Temple Mount and not the

"From above the horse gate repaired the priests, every one over against his house. After them repaired Zadok the son of Immer over against his house. After him repaired also Shemaiah the son of Shechaniah, the keeper of the east gate. After him repaired Hananiah the son of Shelemiah, and Hanun the sixth son of Zalaph, another piece. After him repaired Meshullam the son of Berechiah over against his chamber."

(Neh. 3:28–30)

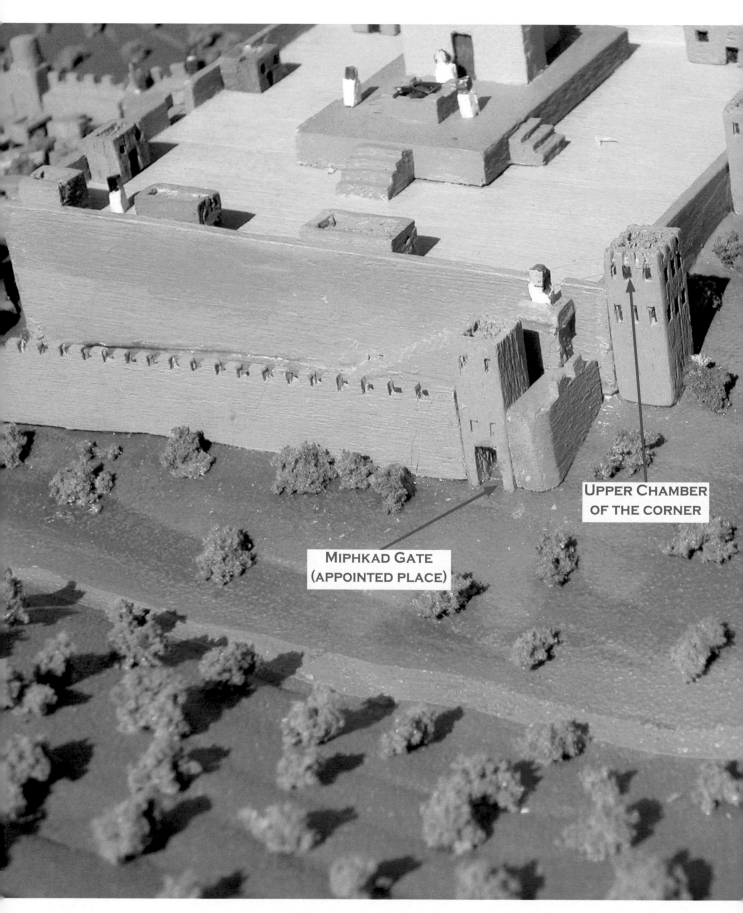

UPPER CHAMBER
OF THE CORNER

MIPHKAD GATE
(APPOINTED PLACE)

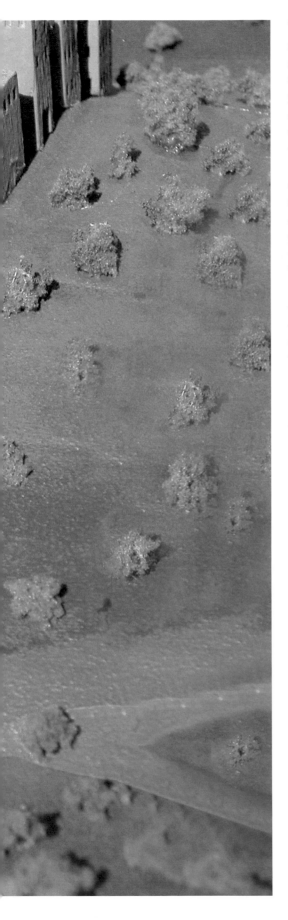

Temple Mount wall itself, as was the case in some of the other periods. When digging in front of the Golden Gate, Charles Warren accidentally found a massive masonry wall. This wall, which curves round to meet the Temple Mount wall at the northeastern corner, appears to date from the Iron Age period.

The stretch of wall between the Horse Gate and the Miphkad Gate sought by Charles Warren was not found in his extensive tunnelling operations. The rubble and shingle which he did find indicated that the wall of Nehemiah had been completely dismantled in 70 A.D. (Herod used mostly old walls on which to build.) It was only in the Byzantine period that the city wall joined the Temple Mount wall at the southeast corner. Warren's Shaft at the southeast corner made it quite clear that a city wall was never previously attached to the Temple Mount as the city wall was considered to be profane.

THE PLACE OF THE NETHINIMS (Neh. 3:31)

The place (in Hebrew, *beth* = "house") of the Nethinims or temple-servants would logically have belonged here, close to the Temple Mount. The merchants must also have had a communal building of some sort in this area.

THE GATE MIPHKAD AND THE GOING UP OF THE CORNER

We first deal with the "going up of the corner." As a rule, the word for "going up, *aliyah* in Hebrew, is translated as "chamber" in the Bible and in one case (2 Sam. 18:33), refers to an upper chamber or gate. It could therefore also refer to an upper chamber of a gate. While tracing the outline of the pre-exilic Temple Mount, which was a square of 500 cubits (262.50 m; *Middot* 2:1), Leen Ritmeyer discovered that the east-

(opposite) "After him repaired Malchiah the goldsmith's son unto the place of the Nethinims, and of the merchants, over against the gate Miphkad, and to the going up of the corner." (Neh. 3:31)

This model of the Herodian Temple Mount shows the Miphkad Gate in the city wall, with steps leading down into the Kidron Valley. The eastern gate of the Temple Mount was known as the Shushan Gate.

ern wall of this Temple Mount extended some 39 feet (12 m) to the north of the square Temple platform. This extension belonged no doubt to the northern fortification of the Temple Mount, which had towers built into it, as we have already seen at the northwestern corner where the towers of Hananeel and Meah were located. These towers, in order to be effective, were several stories high. We suggest that the "going up" of Nehemiah 3:31 refers to the upper chamber of a defensive tower at the

northeast corner, the remains of which can still be seen today.

The gate Miphkad is mentioned before this upper chamber and must therefore have been located in the city wall, just before it curves round to join up with the Temple Mount near the upper chamber. This very wide curved section was unexpectedly found by Warren, when tunnelling towards the Golden Gate.

This Miphkad gate would have been located in the city wall and near the

Eastern (Shushan) Gate of the Temple Mount. We imagine a flight of steps leading down from the Shushan Gate to the Miphkad Gate.

The eastern gate of the Temple Mount has always been associated with the scapegoat and the red heifer. The monolithic gateposts, discovered by De Vogüé inside the Golden Gate in 1864, have been identified by Ritmeyer as the gateposts of the Shushan Gate. The city wall, the towers and a causeway which

The Golden Gate, site of the ancient Shushan Gate, on the eastern side of the Temple Mount. Today this gate is permanently sealed.

Model of the Herodian Temple Mount showing the Miphkad Gate at bottom left of photograph. This is a reconstructed form of the eastern gate which in its original form dates back to the time of Hezekiah.

was later built from the eastern gate to the Mount of Olives are mentioned together in the Mishnah (*Shekalim* 4:2 and *Parah* 3:6). To go from the Temple Mount to the Mount of Olives necessitates a gate in the eastern city wall, which must have been called the Miphkad Gate in the time of Nehemiah.

In this stretch of city wall just to the north of the Golden Gate, remains of the Corner Tower mentioned in Nehemiah 3:31 are visible. Leen Ritmeyer has identified the lowest stone courses here, with their rough bosses, as part of a tower which projected outwards towards the north from the original 500-cubit-square Temple platform. The upper stone courses date from the Islamic and Turkish periods. The three large stones on immediate right are Herodian.

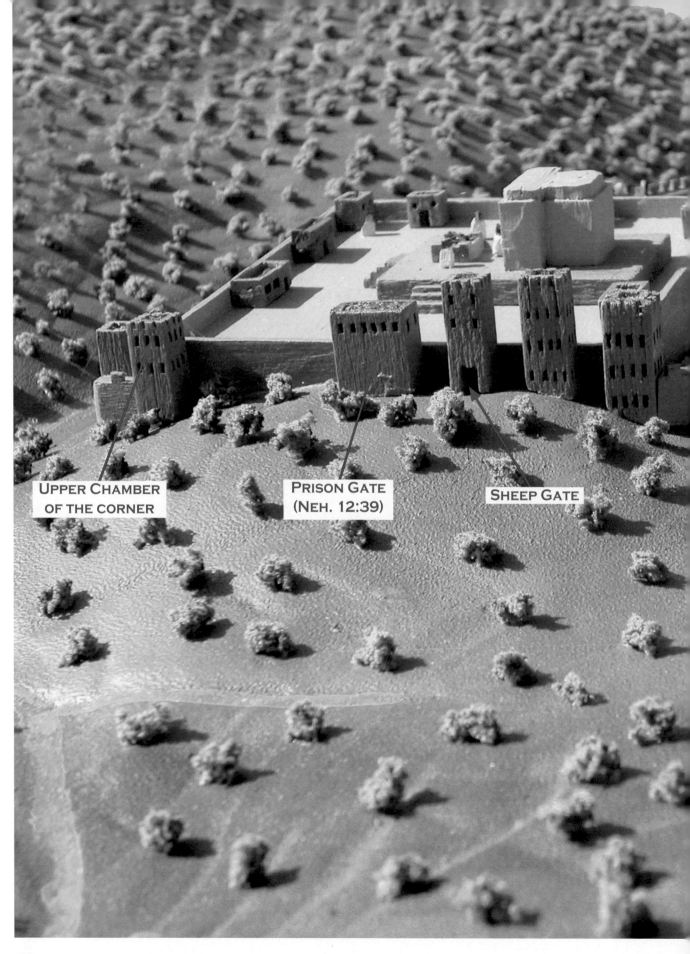

UPPER CHAMBER
OF THE CORNER

PRISON GATE
(NEH. 12:39)

SHEEP GATE

And from above the gate of Ephraim, and above the old gate, and above the fish gate, and the tower of Hananeel, and the tower of Meah, even unto the sheep gate: and they stood still in the prison gate.

(Neh. 12:39)

THE PRISON GATE

In the record of the circuit, which, of course, goes in the opposite direction to that of Nehemiah 3, the Sheep Gate and the Prison (Matarah) Gate in Nehemiah 12:39 are mentioned after the towers of Hananeel and Meah and this is where the two companies stood still to give thanks. This was obviously a different prison to that in the Court of the Prison.

Archaeological evidence for this tower may exist in the northern wall of the square Temple Mount in the so-called Tank 29, which was excavated by Warren. The southern piers of this medieval structure are cut out of bedrock and may belong to an earlier structure which projected to the north of the wall of the raised platform. Tank 29, with its bedrock-cut cells, would have been suitable for use as a prison. If this feature indeed points to the former location of the Prison Gate, then, following the circuit described in Neh. 12, where the Sheep Gate precedes that of the Prison Gate, the latter and the twin towers of Hananeel and Meah would have flanked this same Sheep Gate.

AND BETWEEN THE GOING UP OF THE CORNER UNTO THE SHEEP GATE REPAIRED THE GOLDSMITHS AND THE MERCHANTS.
(NEH. 3:32)

It is said that the pursuit of noble activity is far more gratifying than the pursuit of pleasure. For such a sense of satisfaction for a task accomplished, the meeting of the two companies here above the Prison Gate would rival that of the meeting of the two teams of builders of Hezekiah's Tunnel some centuries earlier. It is one of the delights of Jerusalem archaeology that through its stones and dust we can reproduce in our imagination those scenes of Bible times and "hear the joy of Jerusalem afar off" (Neh. 12:43).

(right) Jerusalem in the time of Nehemiah. Note the two companioes walking on the walls in opposite directions to meet up over the Prison Gate.

(below) The city of Nehemiah in relation to the Old City of today.

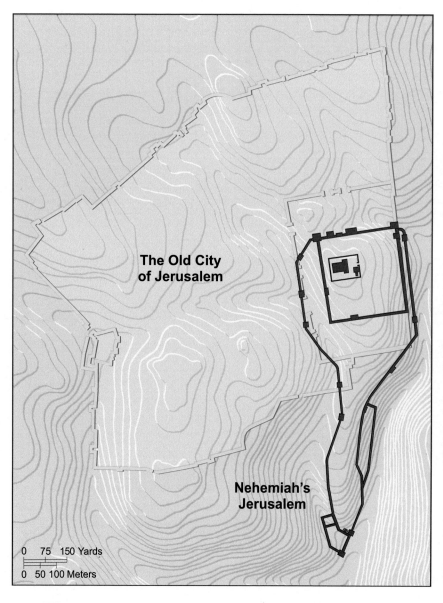

The Old City of Jerusalem

Nehemiah's Jerusalem

0   75   150 Yards

0   50 100 Meters

NEHEMIAH 12:27–43

And at the dedication of the wall of Jerusalem they sought the Levites out of all their places, to bring them to Jerusalem, to keep the dedication with gladness, both with thanksgivings, and with singing, with cymbals, psalteries, and with harps. And the sons of the singers gathered themselves together, both out of the plain country round about Jerusalem, and from the villages of Netophathi;

Also from the house of Gilgal, and out of the fields of Geba and Azmaveth: for the singers had builded them villages round about Jerusalem. And the priests and the Levites purified themselves, and purified the people, and the gates, and the wall.

Then I brought up the princes of Judah upon the wall, and appointed two great companies of them that gave thanks, whereof one went on the right hand upon the wall toward the dung gate:

And after them went Hoshaiah, and half of the princes of Judah, and Azariah, Ezra, and Meshullam, Judah, and Benjamin, and Shemaiah, and Jeremiah, and certain of the priests' sons with trumpets; namely, Zechariah the son of Jonathan, the son of Shemaiah, the son of Mattaniah, the son of Michaiah, the son of Zaccur, the son of Asaph:

And his brethren, Shemaiah, and Azarael, Milalai, Gilalai, Maai, Nethaneel, and Judah, Hanani, with the musical instruments of David the man of God, and Ezra the scribe before them. And at the fountain gate, which was over against them, they went up by the stairs of the city of David, at the going up of the wall, above the house of David, even unto the water gate eastward.

And the other company of them that gave thanks went over against them, and I after them, and the half of the people upon the wall, from beyond the tower of the furnaces even unto the broad wall; And from above the gate of Ephraim, and above the old gate, and above the fish gate, and the tower of Hananeel, and the tower of Meah, even unto the sheep gate: and they stood still in the prison gate.

So stood the two companies of them that gave thanks in the house of God, and I, and the half of the rulers with me: And the priests; Eliakim, Maaseiah, Miniamin, Michaiah, Elioenai, Zechariah, and Hananiah, with trumpets; And Maaseiah, and Shemaiah, and Eleazar, and Uzzi, and Jehohanan, and Malchijah, and Elam, and Ezer. And the singers sang loud, with Jezrahiah their overseer. Also that day they offered great sacrifices, and rejoiced: for God had made them rejoice with great joy: the wives also and the children rejoiced: so that the joy of Jerusalem was heard even afar off.